Contents

Chapter 1

Black Friday (shopping)

For other events, see List of Black Fridays.

Black Friday is the Friday following Thanksgiving Day in the United States (the fourth Thursday of November). Since the early 2000s, it has been regarded as the beginning of the Christmas shopping season in the US, and most major retailers open very early (and more recently during overnight hours) and offer promotional sales. Black Friday is not an official holiday, but California and some other states observe "The Day After Thanksgiving" as a holiday for state government employees, sometimes in lieu of another federal holiday such as Columbus Day.[1] Many non-retail employees and schools have both Thanksgiving and the following Friday off, which, along with the following regular weekend, makes it a four-day weekend, thereby increasing the number of potential shoppers. It has routinely been the busiest shopping day of the year since 2005,[2] although news reports, which at that time were inaccurate,[3] have described it as the busiest shopping day of the year for a much longer period of time.[4] Similar stories resurface year upon year at this time, portraying hysteria and shortage of stock, creating a state of positive feedback.

In 2014, $50.9 billion was spent during the 4-day Black Friday weekend, down 11% from last year. While approximately 133 million U.S. consumers shopped during the same period, down 5.2% from last year's 141 million.

The day's name originated in Philadelphia, where it originally was used to describe the heavy and disruptive pedestrian and vehicle traffic that would occur on the day after Thanksgiving.[5][6] Use of the term started before 1961 and began to see broader use outside Philadelphia around 1975. Later an alternative explanation was made: that retailers traditionally operated at a financial loss ("in the red") from January through November, and "Black Friday" indicates the point at which retailers begin to turn a profit, or "in the black".[5][7]

For many years, it was common for retailers to open at 6:00 a.m., but in the late 2000s many had crept to 5:00 or even 4:00. This was taken to a new extreme in 2011, when several retailers (including Target, Kohl's, Macy's, Best Buy, and Bealls[8]) opened at midnight for the first time.[9] In 2012, Walmart and several other retailers announced that they would open most of their stores at 8:00 p.m. on Thanksgiving Day (except in states where opening on Thanksgiving is prohibited due to blue laws, such as Massachusetts where they still opened around midnight),[10] prompting calls for a walkout among some workers.[11] In 2014 stores such as JCPenney, Best Buy, and Radio Shack opened at 5 PM on Thanksgiving Day while stores such as Target, Walmart, Belk, and Sears opened at 6 PM on Thanksgiving Day.[12][13][14] There have been reports of violence occurring between shoppers on Black Friday.

It is common for prospective shoppers to camp out over the Thanksgiving holiday in an effort to secure a place in front of the line and thus a better chance at getting desired items; because this poses a significant safety risk (such as the use of propane and generators in the most elaborate cases, and in general, the blocking of emergency access and fire lanes) at least one city has banned this practice.[15]

1.1 Shopping

1

1.1.1   United States

A crowded shopping center on Black Friday

The states which have official public holidays for state government employees on "The Day After Thanksgiving" include Arkansas, California, Delaware, Florida, Georgia, Illinois, Indiana, Iowa, Kentucky, Maine, Maryland, Michigan, Minnesota, Nebraska, Nevada, New Hampshire, New Mexico, Ohio, Oklahoma, Pennsylvania, South Carolina, Texas, Washington, West Virginia and Wisconsin.

The news media have long described the day after Thanksgiving as the busiest shopping day of the year.*[4] In earlier years, this was not actually the case. In the period from 1993 through 2001, for example, Black Friday ranked from fifth to tenth on the list of busiest shopping days, with the last Saturday before Christmas usually taking first place.*[3] In 2003, however, Black Friday actually was the busiest shopping day of the year, and it has retained that position every year since, with the exception of 2004, when it ranked second (after Saturday, December 18).*[2]

The SouthPark neighborhood of Charlotte, North Carolina, is the most trafficked area of the United States on Black Friday.*[16]*[17]

Black Friday is popular as a shopping day for a combination of reasons. As the first day after the last major holiday before Christmas it marks the unofficial beginning of the Christmas season. Additionally, many employers give their employees the day off as part of the Thanksgiving holiday weekend. In order to take advantage of this, virtually all retailers in the country, big and small, offer various sales including limited amounts of doorbuster/doorcrasher items to entice traffic. Recent years have seen retailers extend beyond normal hours in order to maintain an edge, or to simply keep up with the competition. Such hours may include opening as early as 12:00 am or remaining open overnight on Thanksgiving Day and beginning sale prices at midnight. In 2010, Toys 'R' Us began their Black Friday sales at 10:00 pm on Thanksgiving Day and further upped the ante by offering free boxes of Crayola crayons and coloring books for as long as supplies lasted. Other retailers, like Sears, Express, MK, Victoria Secret, Zumiez, Tilly's, American Eagle, Nike, Jordan, Puma,

Aéropostale, and Kmart, began Black Friday sales early Thanksgiving morning, and ran them through as late as 11:00 pm Friday evening. Forever 21 went in the opposite direction, opening at normal hours on Friday, and running late sales until 2:00 am Saturday morning.[18][19] Historically, it was common for Black Friday sales to extend throughout the following weekend. However, this practice has largely disappeared in recent years, perhaps because of an effort by retailers to create a greater sense of urgency.

The news media usually give heavy play to reports of Black Friday shopping and their implications for the commercial success of the Christmas shopping season, but the relationship between Black Friday sales and retail sales for the full holiday season is quite weak and may even be negative.[20]

On 23 April 2014, *.blackfriday* joined a growing list of ICANN top-level domains (such as—traditionally -- .com, .net, and .org).[21][22]

1.1.2 Canada

The large population centers on Lake Ontario in Canada have always attracted cross-border shopping into the US states, and as Black Friday became more popular in the US, Canadians often flocked to the US because of their lower prices and a stronger Canadian dollar. After 2001, many were traveling for the deals across the border. Starting in 2008 and 2009, due to the parity of the Canadian dollar compared with the American dollar, several major Canadian retailers ran Black Friday deals of their own to discourage shoppers from leaving Canada.[23][24]

The year 2012 saw the biggest Black Friday to date in Canada, as Canadian retailers embraced it in an attempt to keep shoppers from travelling across the border.[25]

Before the advent of Black Friday in Canada, the most comparable holiday was Boxing Day in terms of retailer impact and consumerism. Black Fridays in the US seem to provide deeper or more extreme price cuts than Canadian retailers, even for the same international retailer.

1.1.3 Mexico

In Mexico, Black Friday was the inspiration for the government and retailing industry to create an annual weekend of discounts and extended credit terms, El Buen Fin, meaning "the good weekend" in Spanish.[26] El Buen Fin has been in existence since 2011 and takes place on November in the weekend prior to the Monday in which the Mexican Revolution holiday is pushed from its original date of November the 20th, as a result of the measure taken by the government of pushing certain holidays to the Monday of their week in order to avoid the workers and students to make a " larger" weekend (for example, not attending in a Friday after a Thursday holiday, thus making a 4-day weekend). On this weekend, major retailers extend their store hours[27] and offer special promotions, including extended credit terms and price promotions.

1.1.4 India

The popularity of Black Friday is also increasing in India. The reason for this is the growing number of e-commerce websites. The big e-commerce retailers in India are trying to emulate the concept of shopping festivals from the United States like Black Friday and Cyber Monday. Flipkart, Snapdeal and Amazon have been offering discounted products on the major festivals in India. December witnesses the Great Online Shopping Festival (also called GOSF) for three days where people shop from all the major e-commerce players and large FMCG brands.

According to Google Trends, the interest for Black Friday is rising every year. Comparing the search volume of the term Black Friday in November 2012 and November 2013, the increase is almost 50 percent (22,200 is the search volume in November 2012 and 33,100 is the search volume in November 2013, according to the Google Adwords).

1.1.5   Panama

In Panama, Black Friday was first celebrated in 2012, as a move from the Government to attract local tourism to the country's capital city. During its first year it was believed to have attracted an inflow of about 35,000 regional tourists according to the government's immigration census.

1.1.6   United Kingdom

Black Friday also occurs in the United Kingdom. One of the UK's first black Friday events took place in 2003 in Staples Corner London, hosted by UK retailer Currys. The retailers black Friday sale in its Staples Corner outlet sold laptops and other electronic devices for under £50, since then a lot other major online retailers have followed the trend like Amazon, Littlewoods, AO Retail, Cotswold Outdoor and Apple.*[28]*[29] In 2013 Asda (part of Wal-Mart Stores, Inc.) announced its "Walmart's Black Friday by ASDA" campaign promoting the Black Friday concept in the UK. A number of other online and instore companies are now embracing the American tradition, although others appear sceptical, with one trade publication labelling it 'simply an Americanism, which doesn't translate very well.'*[30]

In 2014, more UK-based retailers adopted the 'Black Friday' marketing scheme than ever. Included are ao.com, very.co.uk, John Lewis and Argos. They offer massively discounted prices to entice Christmas shoppers. During Black Friday sales in 2014, police forces were called to stores across the United Kingdom to deal with crowd control issues, assaults, threatening customers and traffic issues.*[31] Sir Peter Fahy, Chief Constable of Greater Manchester Police, stated: "The events of last night were totally predictable and I am disappointed that stores did not have sufficient security staff on duty." *[32] In response to incidents at branches of Tesco, Greater Manchester Police's deputy chief constable Ian Hopkins said that shoppers had behaved in an "appalling" fashion and the lack of planning from retailers was "really disappointing": "They should have planned appropriately with appropriate levels of security to make sure people were safe. They have primary responsibility to keep people safe and they can't rely on the police to turn up and bail them out and that's what happened last night." *[33]

1.1.7   France

French businessmen are slowly inserting the Black Friday consumer craze of the US.*[34] Discounts of up to 85% were given by retailing giants such as Apple and Amazon in 2014.*[35] French electronics retailers such as FNAC and Auchan advertised deals online while Darty also took part in this once a year monster Sale. Retailers favored the very American term "Black Friday" to "Vendredi noir" in their advertisements.*[36]

1.1.8   Other countries

In recent years, Black Friday has been promoted in Australia by online retailers. In 2011, Online Shopping USA hosted an event on Twitter. Twitter users had to use the hashtag #osublackfriday and it allowed them to follow along and tweet favourite deals and discounts from stores.*[37] In 2013, Apple extended its Black Friday deals to Australia. Purchasing online gave customers free shipping and free iTunes gift cards with every purchase. The deals were promoted on their website, it read 'Official Apple Store - One day Apple shopping event Friday, 29 November'.*[38]

In 2012, after two years of disappointing results, several department stores in Brazil joined their foreign competitors in a successful Black Friday which more than doubled the total revenue in comparison to the previous year.

Black Friday is known as *Viernes Negro* in Costa Rica.*[39]

In Germany, Austria and Switzerland, Black Friday Sale is a joint sales initiative by hundreds of online vendors—among them Zalando, Disney Store, Galeria Kaufhof and Sony. Over its first 24-hour run on 28 November 2013, more than 1.2 million people visited the site, making it the single largest online shopping event in German speaking countries.

Starting with 2011 Black Friday become a popular shopping day also in Romania, two major IT&C retailers were the first stores to bring this concept to Romania.*[40]

2014 marked the introduction in Colombia, Bolivia,[*][41] Ireland,[*][42] Denmark, Sweden,[*][43] South Africa,Nigeria,Lebanon and France.[*][44]

1.2   Origin of the term

"Black Friday" as a term has been used in multiple contexts, going back to the nineteenth century,[*][45] where in the United States it was associated with a financial crisis of 1869.

The earliest known usage of "Black Friday" as a post-Thanksgiving shopping day appears in the 1 December 1961 issue of *The Shortsville-Manchester Enterprise* (Shortsville, New York). This article, discovered by Barry Popik, refers to a usage by police in Rochester, New York.

> Kathie Caulkin, our intrepid advertising manager, made a serious mistake in judgment last Friday. Took her three kids to Rochester on the day all city police call "Black Friday." Besides being the day after Thanksgiving -- thus one of the busiest shopping days in the year —bus drivers were still on strike, adding to automotive traffic. Katie reports she waited through 13 changes of a single traffic light —then had to back up to get into the parking garage. "I didn't care if I crumpled fifty fenders at that point," Katie reports.[*][46]

An article mentioning the simultaneous use of the term in Philadelphia appears in a public relations newsletter (18 December 1961). This report notes that, as of that writing, this usage among Philadelphia police officers had already become "customary."

> For downtown merchants throughout the nation, the biggest shopping days normally are the two following Thanksgiving Day. Resulting traffic jams are an irksome problem to the police and, in Philadelphia, it became customary for officers to refer to the post-Thanksgiving days as Black Friday and Black Saturday. Hardly a stimulus for good business, the problem was discussed by the merchants with their Deputy City Representative, Abe S. Rosen, one of the country's most experienced municipal PR executives. He recommended adoption of a positive approach which would convert Black Friday and Black Saturday to Big Friday and Big Saturday.[*][47]

The attempt to rename Black Friday was unsuccessful, and its continued use is shown in a 1966 publication on the day's significance in Philadelphia:

> JANUARY 1966 – "Black Friday" is the name which the Philadelphia Police Department has given to the Friday following Thanksgiving Day. It is not a term of endearment to them. "Black Friday" officially opens the Christmas shopping season in Center City, and it usually brings massive traffic jams and over-crowded sidewalks as the downtown stores are mobbed from opening to closing.[*][6]

The term "Black Friday" began to get wider exposure around 1975, as shown by two newspaper articles from November 29, 1975, both datelined Philadelphia. The first reference is in an article entitled "Army vs. Navy: A Dimming Splendor" , in *The New York Times*:

> Philadelphia police and bus drivers call it "Black Friday" – that day each year between Thanksgiving Day and the Army–Navy Game. It is the busiest shopping and traffic day of the year in the Bicentennial City as the Christmas list is checked off and the Eastern college football season nears conclusion.

The derivation is also clear in an Associated Press article entitled "Folks on Buying Spree Despite Down Economy" , which ran in Pennsylvania's *Titusville Herald* on the same day:

> Store aisles were jammed. Escalators were nonstop people. It was the first day of the Christmas shopping season and despite the economy, folks here went on a buying spree... "That's why the bus drivers and cab drivers call today 'Black Friday,'" a sales manager at Gimbels said as she watched a traffic cop trying to control a crowd of jaywalkers. "They think in terms of headaches it gives them."

The term's spread was gradual, however, and in 1985 the *Philadelphia Inquirer* reported that retailers in Cincinnati and Los Angeles were still unaware of the term.[48]

1.2.1 Accounting practice

Many merchants objected to the use of a negative term to refer to one of the most important shopping days in the year.[48] By the early 1980s, an alternative theory began to be circulated: that retailers traditionally operated at a financial loss for most of the year (January through November) and made their profit during the holiday season, beginning on the day after Thanksgiving.[5] When this would be recorded in the financial records, once-common accounting practices would use red ink to show negative amounts and black ink to show positive amounts. Black Friday, under this theory, is the beginning of the period when retailers would no longer have losses (the red) and instead take in the year's profits (the black).[49] The earliest known use that presents the "black ink theory" appeared in the November 28, 1981 edition of the *Philadelphia Inquirer*:

> If the day is the year's biggest for retailers, why is it called Black Friday? Because it is a day retailers make profits – black ink, said Grace McFeeley of Cherry Hill Mall. "I think it came from the media," said William Timmons of Strawbridge & Clothier. "It's the employees, we're the ones who call it Black Friday," said Belle Stephens of Moorestown Mall. "We work extra hard. It's a long hard day for the employees." [50]

This, like the 1961 and 1966 examples from Philadelphia, above, was found by Bonnie Taylor-Blake of the American Dialect Society.

The Christmas shopping season is of enormous importance to American retailers and, while most retailers intend to and actually do make profits during every quarter of the year, some retailers are so dependent on the Christmas shopping season that the quarter including Christmas produces all the year's profits and compensates for losses from other quarters.[51]

1.3 Violence and chaos

In 2006, a man shopping at Best Buy was recorded on video assaulting another shopper.[52] Unruly Walmart shoppers at a store outside Columbus, Ohio, quickly flooded in the doors at opening, pinning several employees against stacks of merchandise.[53] Nine shoppers in a California mall were injured, including an elderly woman who had to be taken to the hospital, when the crowd rushed to grab gift certificates that had been released from the ceiling.[54]

In 2008, a crowd of approximately 2,000 shoppers in Valley Stream, New York, waited outside for the 5:00 am opening of the local Wal-Mart. As opening time approached, the crowd grew anxious and when the doors were opened the crowd pushed forward, breaking the door down, and trampling a 34-year-old employee to death. The shoppers did not appear concerned with the victim's fate, expressing refusal to halt their stampede when other employees attempted to intervene and help the injured employee, complaining that they had been waiting in the cold and were not willing to wait any longer. Shoppers had begun assembling as early as 9:00 PM the evening before. Even when police arrived and attempted to render aid to the injured man, shoppers continued to pour in, shoving and pushing the officers as they made their way into the store. Several other people incurred minor injuries, including a pregnant woman who had to be taken to the hospital.[55][56][57] The incident may be the first case of a death occurring during Black Friday sales; according to the National Retail Federation, "We are not aware of any other circumstances where a retail employee has died working on the day after Thanksgiving." [55]

On the same day, two people were fatally shot during an altercation at a Toys 'r Us in Palm Desert, California.[55]

During Black Friday 2010, a Madison, Wisconsin woman was arrested outside of a Toys 'R' Us store after cutting in line, and threatening to shoot other shoppers who tried to object.[58] A Toys for Tots volunteer in Georgia was stabbed by a shoplifter.[59] An Indianapolis woman was arrested after causing a disturbance by arguing with other Wal-Mart shoppers. She had been asked to leave the store, but refused.[60] A man was arrested at a Florida Wal-Mart on drug and weapons charges after other shoppers waiting in line for the store to open noticed that he was carrying a handgun and reported the matter to police. He was discovered to also be carrying two knives and a pepper spray grenade.[61] A man in Buffalo, New York, was trampled when doors opened at a Target store and unruly shoppers rushed in, in an episode reminiscent of the deadly 2008 Wal-Mart stampede.*[62]

On Black Friday 2011, a woman at a Porter Ranch, California Walmart used pepper spray on fellow shoppers, causing minor injuries to a reported 20 people who had been waiting hours for the store to open. The incident started as people waited in line for the newly discounted Xbox 360. A witness said a woman with two children in tow became upset with the way people were pushing in line. The witness said she pulled out pepper spray and sprayed the other people in line. Another account stated: "The store had brought out a crate of discounted Xbox 360s, and a crowd had formed to wait for the unwrapping, when the woman began spraying people 'in order to get an advantage,' according to the police."*[63] In an incident outside a Walmart store in San Leandro, California, one man was wounded after being shot following Black Friday shopping at about 1:45 am.*[64]

Also stemming from Black Friday unruliness in 2011, 73-year-old greeter Jan Sullivan was fired from a Tampa area Wal-Mart after she was shoved by a Black Friday shopper. Sullivan alleges that when she attempted to stop an unnamed woman from exiting through a door where exits were not being permitted, the woman pushed her. Sullivan claims that as she fell, she instinctively tried to grab onto the woman to keep from falling. Since Wal-Mart employees are not allowed to touch customers, Sullivan was then fired. The story has been a source of some controversy for Wal-Mart and garnered much community support for Sullivan, including media coverage and at least two Indiegogo fundraisers were launched to support her financially after the incident.*[65]

On Black Friday 2012, two people were shot outside a Wal-Mart in Tallahassee, Florida during a dispute over a parking space.*[66]

On Black Friday in 2013, a person in Las Vegas who was carrying a big-screen TV home from a Target store on Thanksgiving was shot in the leg as he tried to wrestle the item back from a robber who had just stolen it from him at gunpoint.*[67] In Romeoville IL, a police officer shot a suspected shoplifter driving a car that was dragging a fellow officer at a Kohl's department store. The suspect and the dragged officer were treated for shoulder injuries. Three people were arrested.*[68]

At the Franklin Mills Mall in Philadelphia a fight was caught on camera in which a woman was taken to the ground. The video also caught a separate possibly related fight happening simultaneously.*[69]

1.4 History

The day after Thanksgiving as the unofficial start of the holiday shopping season may be linked together with the idea of Santa Claus parades. Parades celebrating Thanksgiving often include an appearance by Santa at the end of the parade, with the idea that 'Santa has arrived' or 'Santa is just around the corner' because Christmas is always the next major holiday following Thanksgiving.

In the late 19th and early 20th centuries, many Santa or Thanksgiving Day parades were sponsored by department stores. These included the Toronto Santa Claus Parade, in Canada, sponsored by Eaton's, and the Macy's Thanksgiving Day Parade sponsored by Macy's. Department stores would use the parades to launch a big advertising push. Eventually it just became an unwritten rule that no store would try doing Christmas advertising before the parade was over. Therefore, the day after Thanksgiving became the day when the shopping season officially started.

Later on, the fact that this marked the official start of the shopping season led to controversy. In 1939, retail shops would have liked to have a longer shopping season, but no store wanted to break with tradition and be the one to start advertising before Thanksgiving. President Franklin D. Roosevelt moved the date for Thanksgiving one week earlier, leading to much anger by the public who wound up having to change holiday plans.*[70] Some even refused the change, resulting in the U.S. citizens celebrating Thanksgiving on two separate days.*[70] Some started referring to the change as Franksgiving.

1.5 Controversy

The sale day has caused a number of controversies over various practices:

- Making unreasonable demands on staff, including requiring them to work, often long shifts, during Thanksgiving.

- Health and safety risks due to insufficient staff for crowd management.

- Selling "derivative" products manufactured just for Black Friday with lower specifications.*[71]

1.6 Gray Thursday

Gray Thursday, Walmart

In recent years, retailers have been trending towards opening on **Gray Thursday**, occurring Thanksgiving evening. In 2011, Walmart began its holiday sale at 10 p.m. on Thanksgiving Day for the first time. In 2012, Walmart began its Black Friday sales at 8 p.m. the day before on Thanksgiving; stores that are normally open 24 hours a day on a regular basis started their sales at this time, while stores that do not have round-the-clock shopping hours opened at 8 p.m. Competitors Sears and Kmart also opened at 8 p.m. on Thursday night, while Target and Toys "R" Us opened at 9 p.m. Other retailers, such as Lord & Taylor opened on Thanksgiving for the first time.*[72]*[73] In 2013, more retailers announced plans to open earlier on Thanksgiving. Kmart planned to open at 6 a.m. Thanksgiving and stay open for 41 consecutive hours until 11 p.m. Friday. Toys "R" Us opened at 5 p.m. on Thanksgiving. Walmart planned to start Black Friday sales at 6 p.m. on Thanksgiving while Best Buy planned to open at 6 p.m. JCPenney, Kohl's, Macy's, Sears, and Target planned to open at 8 p.m. on Thanksgiving.*[74] In addition, Simon Property Group planned to open its malls at 8 p.m. on Thanksgiving.*[75] 15,000 consumers "stormed the entrances" at Macy's Herald Square for the 8:00 PM opening on Thursday.*[76]

A number of media sources began referring to this instead by either the name **Black Thursday***[77]*[78] or **Brown Thursday.***[79]

The 2014 "Gray Thursday" sales were, in general, a failure, as overall sales for the holiday weekend fell 11% compared to the previous year despite heavy traffic at the stores on Thanksgiving night.*[80]

1.7 Online

1.7.1 Advertising tip sites

Some websites offer information about day-after-Thanksgiving specials up to a month in advance. The text listings of items and prices are usually accompanied by pictures of the actual ad circulars. These are either leaked by insiders or intentionally released by large retailers to give consumers insight and allow them time to plan.

In recent years, some retailers (including Walmart, Target, OfficeMax, Big Lots, and Staples) have claimed that the advertisements they send in advance of Black Friday and the prices included in those advertisements are copyrighted and are trade secrets.*[81]

Some of these retailers have used the take-down system *[82]of the Digital Millennium Copyright Act as a means to remove the offending price listings. This policy may come from the fear that competitors will slash prices, and shoppers may comparison shop. The actual validity of the claim that prices form a protected work of authorship is uncertain as the prices themselves (though not the advertisements) might be considered a fact in which case they would not receive the same level of protection as a copyrighted work.*[83]

The benefit of threatening Internet sites with a DMCA based lawsuit has proved tenuous at best. While some sites have complied with the requests, others have either ignored the threats or simply continued to post the information under the name of a similar sounding fictional retailer. However, careful timing may mitigate the take-down notice. An Internet service provider in 2003 brought suit against Best Buy, Kohl's, and Target Corporation, arguing that the take-down notice provisions of the DMCA are unconstitutional. The court dismissed the case, ruling that only the third-party posters of the advertisements, and not the ISP itself, would have standing to sue the retailers.*[84]

Usage of Black Friday Advertising Tip sites*[85] and buying direct varies by state in the U.S., influenced in large part by differences in shipping costs and whether a state has a sales tax. However, in recent years, the convenience of online shopping has increased the number of cross-border shoppers seeking bargains from outside of the U.S., especially from Canada. Statistics Canada indicates that online cross-border shopping by Canadians has increased by about 300M a year since 2002.*[86] The complex nature of additional fees such as taxes, duties and brokerage can make calculating the final cost of cross-border Black Friday deals difficult. Dedicated cross-border shopping solutions such as the Canadian shopping platform Wishabi*[87] and Canada Post's Borderfree exist to mitigate the problem through estimation of the various cost involved.

1.7.2 Cyber Monday

Main article: Cyber Monday

The term *Cyber Monday*, a neologism invented in 2005 by the National Retail Federation's division Shop.org,*[88] refers to the Monday immediately following Black Friday based on a trend that retailers began to recognize in 2003 and 2004. Retailers noticed that many consumers, who were too busy to shop over the Thanksgiving weekend or did not find what they were looking for, shopped for bargains online that Monday from home or work. In 2010, Hitwise reported that:*[89]

> Thanksgiving weekend offered a strong start, especially as Black Friday sales continued to grow in popularity. For the 2nd consecutive year, Black Friday was the highest day for retail traffic during the holiday season, followed by Thanksgiving and Cyber Monday. The highest year-over-year increases in visits took place on Cyber Monday and Black Friday with growth of 16% and 13%, respectively.

In 2013, Cyber Monday online sales grew by 18% over the previous year, hitting a record $1.73 billion, with an average order value of $128.*[90] In 2014, Cyber Monday was the busiest day of the year with sales exceeding $2 billion in desktop online spending, up 17% from the previous year.*[91]

1.7.3 Cyber Week

As reported in the *Forbes* "Entrepreneurs" column on December 3, 2013: "Cyber Monday, the online counterpart to Black Friday, has been gaining unprecedented popularity – to the point where Cyber Sales are continuing on throughout the week." *[92] Peter Greenberg, Travel Editor for CBS News, further advises: "If you want a real deal on Black Friday, stay away from the mall. Black Friday and Cyber Monday are all part of Cyber Week [...]"*[93]

1.8 Retail sales

The National Retail Federation releases figures on the sales for each Thanksgiving weekend. The Federation's definition of "Black Friday weekend" includes Thursday, Friday, Saturday and projected spending for Sunday. The survey estimates number of shoppers, not number of people.

The length of the shopping season is not the same across all years: the date for Black Friday varies between 23 and 29 November, while Christmas Eve is fixed at 24 December. 2012 had the longest shopping season since 2007.*[94]

1.9 See also

- "Black Friday" (*South Park*)

- Black Friday Sale

- Buy Nothing Day

- Cyber Monday

- Giving Tuesday

- Green Monday

- Singles Day, also known as 11.11 (November 11), a day for unmarried people popular among Chinese youth, but promoted by Alibaba Group as an online shopping day. Alibaba reported sales of more than $9 billion for November 2014. It is the largest online shopping day in the world.

- Small Business Saturday

- Super Saturday (Panic Saturday)

1.10 References

[1] "Pima County in Arizona Replaces Columbus Day with Black Friday" . *BestBlackFriday.com*. 2013-08-07.

[2] International Council of Shopping Centers. "Holiday Watch: Media Guide 2006 Holiday Facts and Figure" (PDF).; Shopper-Trak, Press Release, ShopperTrak Reports Positive Response to Early Holiday Promotions Boosts Projections for 2010 Holiday Season at the Wayback Machine (archived November 29, 2010) (November 16, 2010).

[3] International Council of Shopping Centers. "Daily Sales Comparison Top Ten Holiday Shopping Days (1996–2001)" (PDF).

[4] *E.g.,* Albert R. Karr, "Downtown Firms Aid Transit Systems To Promote Sales and Build Good Will," *Wall St. J.,* p. 6 (November 26, 1982); Associated Press, "Holiday Shoppers Jam U.S. Stores," *The New York Times*, p. 30 (November 28, 1981).

[5] Ben Zimmer, The Origins of "Black Friday," *Word Routes* (November 25, 2011).

[6] Martin L. Apfelbaum, Philadelphia's "Black Friday," *American Philatelist*, vol. 69, no. 4, p. 239 (Jan. 1966).

[7] Kevin Drum (November 26, 2010). "Black Friday".

[8] Mark Albright. "Holiday shopping strategy guide for Black Friday". *Tampa Bay Times*. Retrieved 2012-01-23.

[9] Sneed, Tierney (November 23, 2011). "Does 'Black Friday' Start Too Early This Year?". *U.S. News & World Report*.

[10] Grinberg, Emmanuella. "Retail employees fight "Black Friday creep"". *CNN.com*. CNN. Retrieved 15 November 2012.

[11] Fox, Emily. "Wal-Mart workers plan Black Friday walkout". *CNNMoney*. CNN. Retrieved 15 November 2012.

[12] http://siliconangle.com/blog/2014/11/26/which-stores-open-early-on-thanksgiving-day-beat-black-friday/

[13] http://www.doorbusters.net/belk/

[14] http://fortune.com/2014/11/03/jc-penney-opening-thanksgiving/

[15] McCool, Tracy (27 November 2014). "No Black Friday camping allowed outside one Best Buy Store". WJW-TV. Retrieved 27 November 2014.

[16] http://www.wcnc.com/story/local/2014/12/01/10757584/

[17] http://www.wfmynews2.com/news/article/200908/176/Charlottes-Southpark-Mall-Ranked-Most-Congested-In-The-Country

[18] Yi, David (November 23, 2010). "Black Friday deals for Target, H&M, Forever21, Old Navy, Radio Shack, and more". *Daily News* (New York).

[19] "Yahoo! Finance – Financially Fit". Financiallyfit.yahoo.com. November 23, 2010. Retrieved 2012-01-02.

[20] Neil Irwin (Nov 23, 2012). "Black Friday is a bunch of meaningless hype, in one chart". *Washington Post*.

[21] Melissa Preddy (9 July 2014). "Fresh peg on new domain names: "dot-vodka," "dot-Christmas," "dot-fail"". Donald W. Reynolds National Center for Business Journalism / Arizona State University. Retrieved 7 August 2014.

[22] "Delegated Strings".

[23] "Canadian retailers test their own Black Friday". *CBC News*. November 27, 2009.

[24] Canadian retailers fight back against Black Friday deals, Toronto Star 2012

[25] Canadian retailers embracing Black Friday to keep shopping dollars on home turf, National Post 2012

[26] "Mexico Introduces its own version of 'Black Friday' – style shopping blitz", *Wall Street Journal*, 2011-11-18, retrieved 2013-06-20

[27] http://www.excelsior.com.mx/node/784759

[28] "Amazon brings Black Friday to the UK". *blu-ray.com*. November 21, 2010.

[29] "Apple's Australian Store discounts most things by around 10 percent, foreshadows Black Friday deals". *engadget.com*. November 25, 2010.

[30] "Comment: Why we should ignore Black Friday in the UK".

[31] "'Black Friday': Police called to supermarket crowds". BBC News. 28 November 2014.

[32] Dearden, Lizzie (28 November 2014). "Black Friday UK: The shops hit by chaos and violence as shopping frenzy sweeps country". The Independent.

[33] Silverman, Rosa (28 November 2014). "Chaos and violence marrs [*sic*] Black Friday across country". The Telegraph.

[34] "Black Friday struggles to seduce French shoppers - The Local". *www.thelocal.fr*. https://plus.google.com/109658666567908793964/. Retrieved 2015-10-29.

[35] ""Black Friday": comment les marques françaises tentent de surfer sur ces soldes à l'américaine". *Le Huffington Post*. Retrieved 2015-10-29.

[36] "Black Friday goes global as retailers import the US spending holiday - CNET". *CNET*. Retrieved 2015-10-29.

[37] "Black Friday shopping live in Australia" . *retailbiz.com*. November 22, 2011.

[38] "Apple's Black Friday deals go live in Australia" . *Sydney Morning Herald*. November 29, 2013.

[39] Clientes esperaban ofertas más agresivas este Viernes Negro La Nación, 2013-11-29. (Spanish)

[40] "Romanian retailers import 'Black Friday' concept" , *El Rancho*, 2011-11-25, retrieved 2014-04-14

[41] http://www.eldeber.com.bo/economia/campana-black-friday-desata-fiebre.html

[42] https://www.irishtimes.com/news/ireland/irish-news/black-friday-ireland-makes-weekend-of-it-1.2019475

[43] "Black Friday i Sverige (Black Friday in Sweden)", *Veckans Affärer*, 2014-11-28, retrieved 2014-11-28

[44] "Le Black Friday s'invite dans les enseignes françaises (Black Friday shows up among French retailers)", *Le Figaro*, 28 November 2014, retrieved 28 November 2014

[45] "snopes.com: How Did 'Black Friday' Get Its Name?<". Retrieved 2014-11-28.

[46] "Around and About," *The Shortsville-Manchester Enterprise* (Shortsville, NY), 1 December 1961, p. 4.

[47] Denny Griswold, *Public Relations News* (Dec. 18, 1961).

[48] Jennifer Lin, Why the Name Black Friday? Uh . . . Well . . ., *Philadelphia Inquirer* (November 30, 1985).

[49] Black Friday FAQ, *BFAds.net*.

[50] Shoppers Flood Stores for "Black Friday," *Philadelphia Inquirer* (November 28, 1981).

[51] *E.g.*, Toys "R" Us, Inc., Annual Report on Form 10-K for the fiscal year ended Feb. 2, 2008, p. 91.

[52] Popken, Ben (November 27, 2006). "Consumers Gone Wild: Roundup Of Black Friday Violence" . The Consumerist. Retrieved 2012-01-02.

[53] Barbaro, Michael (November 25, 2006). "Attention, Holiday Shoppers: We Have Fisticuffs in Aisle 2" . *The New York Times*.

[54]

[55] "Wal-Mart Worker Dies When Shoppers Break Down Doors" . *Fox News*. November 28, 2008.

[56] Gould, Joe; Trapasso, Clare; Schapiro, Rich (November 28, 2008). "Worker dies at Long Island Wal-Mart after being trampled in Black Friday stampede" . *Daily News* (New York). Archived from the original on November 28, 2008.

[57] "Wal-Mart worker dies in rush; two killed at toy store" . *CNN*. November 28, 2008.

[58] "Black Friday shopper accused of gun threat" . *CNN*. November 26, 2010.

[59]

[60] "Woman Arrested In Walmart Black Friday Dispute – Indiana News Story – WRTV Indianapolis" . Theindychannel.com. November 26, 2010. Retrieved 2012-01-02.

[61] WPEC-CBS12.com (November 26, 2010). "Black Friday shopper arrested on weapons, drug charges in Boynton Beach | boynton, arrested, beach – Top Story – WPEC 12 West Palm Beach" . Cbs12.com. Retrieved 2012-01-02.

[62] "Black Friday shoppers trampled in New York" . *CNN*. November 28, 2010.

[63] ROBERT JABLON (November 25, 2011). "Woman pepper sprays other Black Friday shoppers – Yahoo! News". News.yahoo.com. Retrieved 2012-01-02.

[64] Wildermuth, John (November 26, 2011). "Black Friday shopper shot in robbery attempt" . *San Francisco Chronicle*.

[65] Tessa McLean – July 5, 2012 (July 5, 2012). "Black Friday Meant the End of Life as She Knew It for a 73-Year-Old Walmart Greeter" . blackfriday.bradsdeals.com. Retrieved 2012-08-20.

[66] "2 shot at Florida Walmart over parking space, police say" . Fox News. 23 November 2012.

[67] "Shopper carrying TV home from Target shot in Las Vegas" . *Las Vegas Sun*.

[68] Adam, Sege. "Charges filed after shoplifting suspect shot by police" . *Chicago Tribune.*

[69] "Women Get Into Black Friday Stun Gun Fight Inside the Mall" . *YouTube.*

[70] "Congress Establishes Thanksgiving" . Retrieved 2009-11-15.

[71] http://thedailycougar.com/2013/11/26/consumers-think-twice-going-black-friday-deals/

[72] Li, Shan (November 21, 2011). "Black Friday becoming Black Thursday as stores open on Thanksgiving" . *Los Angeles Times.* Retrieved November 22, 2011.

[73] Clifford, Stephanie (November 9, 2012). "Make Room for Deals After Turkey This Year" . *New York Times.* Retrieved November 10, 2011.

[74] "2013 Thanksgiving and Black Friday Store Hours" . Carterville, IL: WSIL-TV. November 12, 2013. Retrieved November 14, 2013.

[75] Davis, Julie (November 12, 2013). "Will You Shop the King of Prussia Mall on Thanksgiving?". *Racked.* Retrieved November 21, 2013.

[76] "Shoppers Throng to Stores" . WWD. November 29, 2013.

[77] Castellano, Anthony (November 22, 2012). "Black Friday Shopping Kicks Off After Thanksgiving Dinner" . *ABC News.* Retrieved November 23, 2012.

[78] Sreenivasan, Hari (November 22, 2012). "How 'Black Friday' Morphed Into 'Gray Thursday'". *PBS.* Retrieved November 23, 2012.

[79] "Punchlines: The new Black Friday is Brown Thursday" . *USA Today.* November 22, 2013. Retrieved November 27, 2013.

[80] Tabuchi, Tiroko (December 1, 2014). "Black Friday Fatigue? Thanksgiving Weekend Sales Slide 11 Percent" . *The New York Times.* Retrieved October 2, 2015.

[81] "Sale fight no fright for area Web site," *Charleston Gazette & Daily Mail* (November 26, 2002).

[82] "Take Down Letters" . *hBlackFridayDeals.com.* 2015-11-01.

[83] *Feist Publications, Inc., v. Rural Telephone Service Co.*, 499 U.S. 340 (1991).

[84] *Fatwallet, Inc. v. Best Buy Enterprises Services*, 2004 WL 793548 (N.D.Ill. 2004).

[85] Black Friday Advertising: "Black Friday Ads" . Retrieved July 24, 2015.

[86] Stats Can: "Canadian Economic Observer" . Retrieved March 18, 2010.

[87] Wishabi: "cross-border shopping" . Retrieved March 18, 2010.

[88] Hof, Robert D. (November 29, 2005). "Cyber Monday, Marketing Myth" . *Business Week.* Retrieved 2012-11-13.

[89] "Hitwise: Retail traffic up throughout holidays" . December 28, 2010.

[90] "Cyber Monday Jumps 18 Percent to $1.73 billion in 2013" . *comscore.com.* 2015-11-01.

[91] "Cyber Monday 2015 Expectations" . *1cybermondaydeals.com.* 2015-11-01.

[92] "Cyber Week: Crash Prevention Tips" . *Forbes.* December 3, 2013.

[93] Peter Greenberg (November 20, 2013). "The Ultimate Guide to Cyber Week Travel Deals: Black Friday, Cyber Monday & More" . *Huffington Post.*

[94] "Black Friday Weekend Shines as Shoppers Line up for Deals" .

[95] http://www.nrf.com/modules.php?name=News&op=viewlive&sp_id=1705

Chapter 2

Black Friday (South Park)

"**Black Friday**" is the seventh episode of the seventeenth season of *South Park*, and the 244th episode of the series overall. It is the first episode of a three-episode story arc, and premiered in the United States on Comedy Central on November 13, 2013. The plot, which employs themes and motifs from the TV series *Game of Thrones* (in a manner similar to the 2002 *Lord of the Rings* parody episode "The Return of the Fellowship of the Ring to the Two Towers"), concerns the characters' anticipation of a Black Friday sale, with Randy Marsh taking a temporary job as a mall security guard to gain an advantage over the holiday shopping crowds, and the children of South Park split into two factions over whether to collectively purchase bargain-priced Xbox One or PlayStation 4 video game consoles to facilitate their online group gaming. The episode's opening title sequence shows the characters dressed in the role-playing garments they wear in the storyline. The story is continued in the follow-up episodes "A Song of Ass and Fire" and "Titties and Dragons".*[1]*[2]

Due to the overwhelming critical acclaim that the episode received, this episode was submitted for, and received, a nomination for the Primetime Emmy Award for Outstanding Animated Program (for Programming Less Than One Hour) at the 66th Primetime Emmy Awards.

2.1 Plot

The security management at South Park Mall briefs its guards on the upcoming Black Friday shopping day, on which people have been seriously injured or killed in the past. The security Captain, a grizzled veteran with a large scar running down his face across his blind left eye, tells the guards that this year, the mall is offering an 80% discount to the first 30 people in the mall, which is certain to again incite violence among shoppers, much to the concern of the guards. Among the guards is Randy Marsh, who has taken the temporary job not to earn extra holiday money as he says, but to acquire the discounts ahead of the crowds that will camp outside the mall.

Meanwhile, the boys of South Park are dressed in medieval garb while engaging in role playing inspired by *Game of Thrones*, and are themselves anticipating Black Friday, which they see as an impending "battle". Cartman informs his classmates of the 80% discount, and says if they work together, they can all purchase one of the new gaming systems together so that they can play online games together. However, the children become split over whether to purchase Xbox Ones or PlayStation 4s (PS4). Kyle and Stan find themselves on opposite sides of the schism, with Kyle allied with Cartman's Xbox One faction, and Stan on the PS4 side, a parting that the two troubled best friends realize will pit them against each other on Black Friday. Butters, newly introduced to *Game of Thrones*, is allied with Cartman, but seems more preoccupied with the show's focus on male nudity over dragons. The two factions then begin recruiting other children to increase their ranks. At stake, according to Stan, is that if one system is purchased in high volume over the other, that system will become the standard, rendering the other one obsolete, as occurred with the videotape format war. Cartman, strolling through the "Garden of Andros" with Kenny, whose character is "Lady McCormick", tells him that they are only recruiting Xbox One loyalists to help them get inside the mall so they can get cheap Xbox Ones. He wants Kenny to use his influence to "take care" of Kyle, should his loyalty to their faction falter. The garden is then revealed to be the elaborately landscaped back yard of an elderly South Park resident, who orders the children to stop trespassing on his property. This gag recurs throughout the three-part storyline, with Cartman playing different participants in the conflict against each other, only for the old man to inform them of this from his window, much to Cartman's irritation.

The mall's security is further daunted by the news that a new Tickle Me Elmo called "Stop Touching Me Elmo" is being released in time for Black Friday, which leads to shoppers camping outside even earlier than anticipated. As Randy peruses the products to purchase that day, the Captain thanks him for his service, telling him that he can tell that Randy took the job because he genuinely cares about people, a compliment that troubles Randy. Meanwhile, the head of Sony learns of Cartman's campaign, and fearing that an Xbox One sell-through would be bad for Sony's image, decides to market a Black Friday bundle to further entice PS4 customers, which includes four game controllers, a map of Japan, a $100 rebate, and the ability to pre-order *Metal Gear Solid V*, dubbed the "Brack Friday Bunduru". To address increasing crowds, the mall's security tries to hand out wristbands so shoppers can hold places in line, but this leads to a brawl in which the Captain is fatally stabbed. Cradling his dying superior, Randy reveals his true motives for having taken the job. The Captain notes that Randy now knows how serious Black Friday is, and peels off the scar over his left eye, revealing it to be a prosthetic appliance. Before expiring, he places it on Randy's face, telling Randy that regardless of his early motives, he is the Captain now, and must now protect the town. Inspired by the new responsibility, Randy tells his fellow guards that they now have work to do. At the same time, Stan rallies his assembled army, telling them that a new leader has joined them to make sure that the winner of the console war is the PS4: Princess McCormick (Kenny).

2.2 Critical reception

"Black Friday" has received critical acclaim. Max Nicholson of IGN gave the episode an 8.7/10 "Great" rating, writing, "Cleverly fusing elements of the Next-Gen Console War with HBO's Game of Thrones, 'Black Friday' was easily one of the best South Park episodes we've seen in Season 17." *[3]

Ryan McGee of The A.V. Club gave the episode an A−, praising the *Game of Thrones* parody, saying, "Why wrap *Game of Thrones* in all this? There's no *real* reason to do so, except that it's really amusing and offers up a great way to frame the overall narrative. What makes the approach really work is that 'Black Friday' is not a one-for-one parody so much as a thematic one." *[4]

2.3 References

[1] Matt Stone and Trey Parker. "Episode 1708 "A Song of Ass and Fire" Press Release". South Park Studios. Retrieved November 10, 2013.

[2] "Episode 1709 "Titties and Dragons" Press Release". South Park Studios. December 1, 2013. Retrieved December 2, 2013.

[3] Nicholson, Max (November 14, 2013). "South Park: 'Black Friday' Review: The Console War is Coming...". IGN.

[4] McGee, Ryan (November 13, 2013). "Black Friday". The A.V. Club.

2.4 External links

- "Black Friday". South Park Studios.

- "Episode 1707 "Black Friday" Press Release". South Park Studios. November 10, 2013.

Chapter 3

Black Friday Sale

Black Friday Sale is a joint sales initiative by hundreds of online vendors in Germany, Austria and Switzerland, inspired by the American Black Friday. The event was first launched on 28 November 2013: Over its 24-hour run, more than 1.2 million people visited the site, making it the single largest online shopping event in German speaking countries. Many leading online retailers such as Zalando, Disney Store, Saturn, Galeria Kaufhof, Deichmann, The Body Shop, Sony, Yves Rocher and Dell participated in the event in 2013.[*][1]

3.1 Reception

Once the Black Friday Sale started at 7 pm on 28 November 2013, more than 50.000 users simultaneously accessed the site, temporarily causing delays and server overloads. The overwhelming numbers of visitors also caused the servers of several online shops, such as the electronics store Saturn, to suffer significant downtime.[*][2] Despite the technical problems, the first Black Friday Sale generated a significant turnover and was considered a notable success by online retailers and organizers alike.[*][3]

3.2 Upcoming events

After successfully launching in 2013, the Black Friday Sale is set to return on 27 November 2014. The organizers expect more than three million visitors. Once more, several hundred leading online vendors will be involved, among them Douglas Holding, HP, Sony, Tally Weijl and Weltbild. eBay and PayPal are also featured as official partners of the event.[*][4]

3.3 References

[1] "German online newspaper Welt". 22 November 2013.

[2] "German online magazine Channel Observer". 2 December 2013.

[3] "German magazine Internet World Business". 4 December 2013.

[4] "German magazine Moebelkultur". 24 September 2014.

3.4 External links

- Official website

Chapter 4

Buy Nothing Christmas

Buy Nothing Christmas is an ongoing protest and reaction to the commercialization of the North American Christmas and holiday season. It started unofficially in 1968, when Ellie Clark and her family decided to publicly disregard the commercial aspects of the Christmas holiday.[*][1] Contemporarily a movement was created to extend Adbusters' Buy Nothing Day into the entire Christmas season.[*][1] Buy Nothing Christmas first became official in 2001 when a small group of Canadian Mennonites created a website and gave the movement a name.[*][2]

4.1 See also

- Festivus
- Gift economy
- *What Would Jesus Buy* (2007 documentary)

4.2 References

[1] http://www.buynothingchristmas.org/about/index.html

[2] Priesnitz, Wendy. "A Buy Nothing Christmas." *Natural Life Magazine*, November/December 2006. Retrieved 27 November 2008.

4.3 External links

- The Buy Nothing Christmas website

Chapter 5

Buy Nothing Day

Buy Nothing Day demonstration in San Francisco, California, November 2000

Buy Nothing Day (**BND**) is an international day of protest against consumerism. In North America, Buy Nothing Day is held on the Friday after U.S. Thanksgiving, concurrent to Black Friday (on Friday, November 28, 2014; November 27, 2015; November 25, 2016; November 24, 2017); elsewhere, it is held the following day, which is the last Saturday in November.*[1]*[2] Buy Nothing Day was founded in Vancouver by artist Ted Dave*[3] and subsequently promoted by *Adbusters* magazine,*[4] based in Canada.

The first Buy Nothing Day was organized in Canada in September 1992 "as a day for society to examine the issue of

18

over-consumption." In 1997, it was moved to the Friday after American Thanksgiving, also called "Black Friday", which is one of the ten busiest shopping days in the United States. In 2000, advertisements by *Adbusters* promoting Buy Nothing Day were denied advertising time by almost all major television networks except for CNN.*[1] Soon, campaigns started appearing in the United States, the United Kingdom, Israel, Austria, Germany, New Zealand, Japan, the Netherlands, France, Norway and Sweden.*[5] Participation now includes more than 65 nations.

5.1 Activities

Various gatherings and forms of protest have been used on Buy Nothing Day to draw attention to the problem of over-consumption:

- Credit card cut up: Participants stand in a shopping mall, shopping center, or store with a pair of scissors and a poster that advertises help for people who want to put an end to mounting debt and extortionate interest rates with one simple cut.

- Free, non-commercial street parties

- Sit-in

- Zombie walk: Participant "zombies" wander around shopping malls or other consumer havens with a blank stare. When asked what they are doing participants describe Buy Nothing Day.

- Whirl-mart: Participants silently steer their shopping carts around a shopping mall or store in a long, baffling conga line without putting anything in the carts or actually making any purchases.

- Public protests

- Wildcat General Strike: A strategy used for the 2009 Buy Nothing Day where participants not only do not buy anything for twenty-four hours but also keep their lights, televisions, computers and other non-essential appliances turned off, their cars parked, and their phones turned off or unplugged from sunrise to sunset.*[2]

- Buy Nothing Day hike: Rather than celebrating consumerism by shopping, participants celebrate The Earth and nature.*[6]

- Buy Nothing Critical Mass: As the monthly Critical Mass bicycle ride often falls on this day or near, rides in some cities acknowledge and celebrate Buy Nothing Day.

- Buy Nothing Day paddle along the San Francisco waterfront. This event is promoted by the Bay Area Sea Kayakers to kayak along the notoriously consumptive San Francisco waterfront.

- The Winter Coat Exchanges that started in Rhode Island and now have locations in Rhode Island, Kentucky, Utah and Oregon in which coats are collected from anyone who wants to donate, and anyone who needs a winter coat is welcome to take one.

5.2 Criticism

While critics of the day charge that Buy Nothing Day simply causes participants to buy the next day,*[7] Adbusters states that it "isn't just about changing your habits for one day" but "about starting a lasting lifestyle commitment to consuming less and producing less waste."

Other campaigns, such as Shift Your Shopping, attempt to redirect spending away from corporate chains and online giants toward locally owned, community-based businesses as a means to combat consumerism. Even some independent business advocates, such as the American Independent Business Alliance, recognize "Black Friday" frenzy does little for independent businesses and instead encourage people to consider giving gifts but not necessarily "things." *[8]

5.3 Renaming

Adbusters has recently renamed the event Occupy Xmas,[*][9] a reference to the Occupy Movement. Buy Nothing Day was first joined with Adbuster's Buy Nothing Christmas campaign. Shortly thereafter, Lauren Bercovitch, the production manager at Adbusters Media Foundation publicly embraced the principles of Occupy Xmas, advocating "something as simple as buying locally—going out and putting money into your local economy—or making your Christmas presents" .[*][10] Previously, the central message of Occupy X-mas and Occupy Christmas differed in that Occupy X-Mas called for a "buy nothing Christmas" [*][11] and Occupy Christmas called for support of local economy, artists, and craftspeople in holiday shopping. The union of these ideologies calls for a Buy Nothing Day to kick off a season of supporting local economy and family.

5.4 See also

- Advent Conspiracy
- Black Friday
- Buy Nothing Christmas
- Car-Free Days
- Culture jamming
- Cyber Monday
- Festivus
- *Homo consumericus*
- Kashless.org
- *The Story of Stuff* (2007 film)

5.5 References

[1] "Buy Nothing Day"*The Guardian.co.uk*

[2] "Buy Nothing Day"*Adbusters.org*

[3] Crook, Barbara. "Can you say bye to buying 1 day a year?" *The Vancouver Sun*. September 25, 1992.

[4] Click Here to Buy Nothing. Joanna Glasner. *Wired*, Nov 22, 2000.

[5] Jonas Lindkvist (1998). "1998, köp-inget-dagen" (in Sweidsh). En köpfri dag. Retrieved 16 August 2015.

[6] Buy Nothing Day hike announcement http://www.backtonatives.org/events.htm

[7] Why I Shop on Buy Nothing Day, TheTyee.ca, 24 November 2006

[8] "Great Gifts Don't Have to Be "Stuff"". American Independent Business Alliance. Retrieved 23 November 2012.

[9] Occupy Xmas, Archived May 17, 2014 at the Wayback Machine

[10] An interview with Lauren Bercovitch

[11] Buy Nothing Christmas

5.6 External links

- The Buy Nothing Day site through the Adbusters Media Foundation
- BND UK information and support for UK campaigners

Chapter 6

Christmas club

The **Christmas club** is a savings program that was first offered by various banks in the United States during the Great Depression. The concept is that bank customers deposit a set amount of money each week into a special savings account, and receive the money back at the end of the year for Christmas shopping.

6.1 Origins

The first known Christmas club started in 1909, when Merkel Landis, treasurer of the Carlisle (Pennsylvania) Trust Company, introduced the first Christmas savings fund. The club generated 350 customers who saved about $28 each, and the money was disbursed on December 1 of that year.*[1] The January 2, 1920, edition of the Belvidere, Illinois Daily Republican announced that the town's State Farmers Bank was encouraging parents to enroll their children in the Christmas Banking Club "to develop self-reliance and the saving habit".

6.2 Promotion

For decades, financial institutions competed for the holiday savings business, offering enticing premiums and advertising items such as tokens. The Dime Saving Bank of Toledo, Ohio, issued a brass token "good for 25 cents in opening a Christmas account" for 1922-1923. There were also numbered tokens issued by the Atlantic Country Trust Co. in Atlantic City, New Jersey, inscribed on the reverse: "Join our Christmas Club and Have Money When You Need It Most." In the February 2006 issue of *Forbes* magazine, business writer James Surowiecki summarized the accounts' appeal: "The popularity of Christmas club accounts isn't a mystery; if their money was in a regular account, people assumed they'd spend it." *[2]

6.3 Drawbacks

Key drawbacks of Christmas club accounts included low interest rates and a high number of restrictions, such as not allowing withdrawals unless fees were paid. The December 23, 1949 episode of the radio program *Life of Riley* highlighted these problems with an episode featuring Chester Riley visiting the bank to withdraw his Christmas club money. Riley had made only one $2 deposit, but the account had accumulated so many fees (for the passbook, for early withdrawal, and for the mailing of reminders) that Riley owed the bank another 25 cents.

Banks also incurred high costs in maintaining the accounts. According to Dennis Halpin, the CEO for the Capital Communications Federal Credit Union, the union had 3,500 Christmas club members in 1984. Each member required a check to be produced, signed, collated, and mailed, only for 70 percent to be returned to the bank to be deposited in another account.

6.4 References

[1] Joseph Nathan Kane, *Famous First Facts*, 4th ed., (Ace Books, 1974) p. 93.

[2] Surowiecki, James. "Bitter Money and Christmas Clubs." Forbes.com. Feb. 14, 2006.

Numismatist, Marilyn A. Reback, pp. 57–60, Volume 119, Number 12, December 2006

Pinckney, Barbara. "Holiday Clubs Endure Despite Waning Popularity." The Business Review (Albany, NY). Nov. 15, 2002. www.bizjournals.com

Sewall, Tim. "Christmas Club According Is Becoming a Thing of the Past." Memphis Business Journal. Dec. 5, 1997. www.bizjournals.com

Slabaugh, Arlie R. Christmas Tokens and Medals. Chicago: Author, 1966. (ANA Library Catalogue No. RM85.C5S5)

Chapter 7

Christmas creep

Christmas creep is a merchandising phenomenon in which merchants and retailers exploit the commercialized status of Christmas by introducing Christmas-themed merchandise or decorations before the traditional start of the holiday shopping season on the day after Thanksgiving.*[1] The term was first used in the mid-1980s.*[2]

7.1 Economic motivation

It is associated with a desire of merchants to take advantage of particularly heavy Christmas-related shopping well before Black Friday in the United States and before Halloween in Canada. The term is not used in the UK and Ireland, where retailers call Christmas the "golden quarter", that is, the three months of October through December is the quarter of the year in which the retail industry hopes to make the most profit.*[3] It can apply for other holidays as well, notably Valentine's Day, Easter and Mother's Day. The motivation for holiday creep is for retailers to lengthen their selling interval for seasonal merchandise in order to maximize profit and to give early-bird shoppers a head start on that holiday. However, it is not clear that this practice has been consistently beneficial for retailers.*[4]

Seasonal creep is not limited to the northern hemisphere winter holiday season and other popular holidays and observances, but is also becoming more common for merchandise associated with a general season of the year. Advertising for winter-, spring-, summer-, and fall-related goods generally now begins midway through the previous season. For example, many supermarkets in the United Kingdom begin selling Easter eggs even before Christmas, and in the US, stores begin selling 4th of July products before Easter, and the next major holiday is marketed as soon as or before the previous has ended.

In Australia, shops have been known to have their Christmas merchandise available as early as late September, because Halloween is not widely celebrated. The department store, David Jones Limited even begins selling Christmas merchandise at the start of September.

7.2 United States

In United States retail, the phenomenon was pioneered by stores like Sam's Club, which introduced early Christmas sales to support resellers. The hardware chain Lowe's followed in 2000 with a policy of setting out Christmas trees and decorations by October 1, mainly because the Halloween and Thanksgiving holidays do not provide enough merchandise or sales to fill retail space between the end of the summer season and the Christmas season. In 2002–2003, Christmas creep accelerated markedly with retailers such as Walmart, J. C. Penney, and Target beginning their Christmas sales in October.*[5] In 2006 the National Retail Federation, an industry trade group, said that 40 percent of consumers planned to start their holiday shopping before Halloween.

7.3   Broadcasting

Christmas creep has also been cited as a phenomenon in radio broadcasting. Prior to the early 21st century, radio stations commonly began adding some Christmas songs to their regular playlists in early December and then playing an all-Christmas playlist on December 24 and 25, but in 2001 some stations began playing an exclusively Christmas format for the entire month of December. In subsequent years, such stations have commonly shifted to an all-Christmas playlist after US Thanksgiving, or even several weeks earlier. A handful of American radio stations*[6] have, since 2006, earned a reputation for regularly switching to Christmas music on November 1, the day after Halloween; as of 2011, this has not become the norm for most of North America (mid-November is the typical start time for Christmas music on most radio stations in the United States and Canada), and it is still extremely rare to hear stations (other than those pulling a stunt between changing formats) change to Christmas music in October.

Some of the channels in the U.S. television cable channel chain Music Choice begin playing Christmas music continually from the end of Halloween up until the first week of January. In 2012, the first Christmas-oriented TV commercial of the year was aired the day before Halloween; in 2014, one was aired a full week before Halloween.

7.4   Christmas in July

During World War II, the United States Postal Service, the U.S. Army and the U.S. Navy teamed up to a launch a Christmas in July campaign designed to gather Christmas cards, letters, and gifts from American families in time to ship them to troops overseas.*[7] Today, organizations around the world take advantage of the Christmas spirit to hold Christmas in July charity campaigns, often associated with retail partners or sponsors.*[8]*[9] Christmas in July is probably best known as a marketing "holiday" used by retailers to push sales and specials.*[7]*[10]

7.5   Parody

This market trend is parodied in the 1974 animated special *It's the Easter Beagle, Charlie Brown*, when the characters go shopping at a department store and discover that it has its Christmas displays up in the middle of April, including a sign forewarning that there were only a mere 246 days left until Christmas. Additionally, in 1973's *A Charlie Brown Thanksgiving*, Sally complains that she was looking for a turkey tree for Thanksgiving but had only found Christmas supplies.

Several songs satirize the phenomenon, including Loudon Wainwright III's "Suddenly It's Christmas" (from his 1993 live album *Career Moves*), Straight No Chaser's "The Christmas Can-Can" (from their 2009 album *Christmas Cheers*), Paul and Storm's "The Way-Too-Early Christmas Song" (from their 2010 album *Do You Like Star Wars?*). Christian singer/songwriter Brandon Heath voiced his feelings on Christmas creep in the song "The Day After Thanksgiving" (from his 2013 album "Christmas Is Here").

In Jim Butcher's 2012 novel *Cold Days*, Santa Claus himself declares that he's drawing the line at Halloween.

7.6   See also

- Mission creep
- Season creep

7.7   References

[1] Siewers, Alf (November 25, 1987). "He's well-suited to enjoying life of Santa" . *Chicago Sun-Times*. Retrieved December 26, 2007. And so does the culture, with a commercializing of himself that Santa deplores even as he has watched the holiday season creep back to Labor Day.

[2] Maxwell, Kerry (September 18, 2006). "Macmillan English Dictionary Word Of The Week Archive – "Christmas creep"". *New Words*. Macmillan Publishers. Retrieved December 26, 2007. The term Christmas creep was first used in the mid-eighties, though gained wider recognition more recently, possibly due to subsequent coinage of the expression mission creep.

[3] Zoe Wood (Tuesday December 21, 2010) Snow chaos raises fears for Christmas dinners minus the trimmings *The Guardian*

[4] "Christmas Creep: The Shopping Season Is Longer, but Is It Better?". *Knowledge@Wharton*. Wharton School of the University of Pennsylvania. March 1, 2006. Retrieved December 27, 2007. ... Wharton marketing scholars and other analysts say an extended Christmas season is something of a mixed bag. It may hold advantages, disadvantages —or even no advantages —for store owners.

[5] *Christmas Creeps Into Stores*, San Diego Union-Tribune, October 25, 2006. Accessed November 18, 2007.

[6] "WGAL News", *Too Early for Christmas Music? Susquehanna Radio station now playing it*, November 20, 2014

[7] Cecil, Sharon. "Christmas in July: real or sweet deal". *Courier-Journal*. Retrieved July 9, 2015.

[8] Caso, Laura (July 9, 2015). "Celebrating Christmas in July at Wolfson Children's Hospital". First Coast News. Retrieved July 9, 2015.

[9] Langley, Kasey. "Christmas in July event helps families across North Alabama". *WHNT News*. Retrieved July 9, 2015.

[10] Lehmann, Rebecca (July 8, 2015). "Skeptical of Black Friday in July sales? Why you should check them out". Christian Science Monitor. Retrieved July 9, 2015.

7.8 Further reading

- Kelly, John (November 20, 2008). "It's Not the Eggnog Talking: Christmas Is Starting Earlier". *Washington Post*. p. B03. Retrieved December 1, 2008.

- Kelly, John (November 24, 2008). "Earlier Christmas Displays Just a Friendly Reminder". *Washington Post*. p. B03. Retrieved December 1, 2008.

Chapter 8

Christmas Day (Trading) Act 2004

The Christmas Day (Trading) Act 2004 (c 26) is an Act of the Parliament of the United Kingdom. It prevents shops over 280 m²/3,000 sq ft from opening on Christmas Day in England and Wales. Shops smaller than the limit are not affected.

The Act was introduced to the House of Commons by Kevan Jones, MP for North Durham as a Private Member's Bill on 7 January 2004.

The aim of the Act was to keep Christmas Day a "special" day, whereby all major retailers would be closed. Although it was traditional for major retailers to close on 25 December, some retailers, such as Woolworths, began to open some stores in the late 1990s. Both religious groups and shop worker unions were against the idea of Christmas openings, leading to pressure on the Government to pass legislation to prevent the practice.

In 2006, the Scottish Parliament debated a similar law that would apply to shops in Scotland. The law was enacted in 2007 and it contained special provisions for New Year's Day retail activities too. *[4]

8.1 References

- Halsbury's Statutes,

[1] The citation of this Act by this short title is authorised by section 6(1) of this Act.

[2] The Christmas Day (Trading) Act 2004, section 6(4)

[3] The Christmas Day (Trading) Act 2004, section 6(3). The Christmas Day (Trading) Act 2004 (Commencement) Order 2004 (S.I. 2004/3235 (C. 143)), article 2

[4] Christmas Day and New Year's Day Trading (Scotland) Act 2007 Accessed January 21, 2013

8.2 External links

- The Christmas Day (Trading) Act 2004, as amended from the National Archives.

- The Christmas Day (Trading) Act 2004, as originally enacted from the National Archives.

- Explanatory notes to the Christmas Day (Trading) Act 2004.

- Department of Trade and Industry Factsheet

Chapter 9

Christmas Price Index

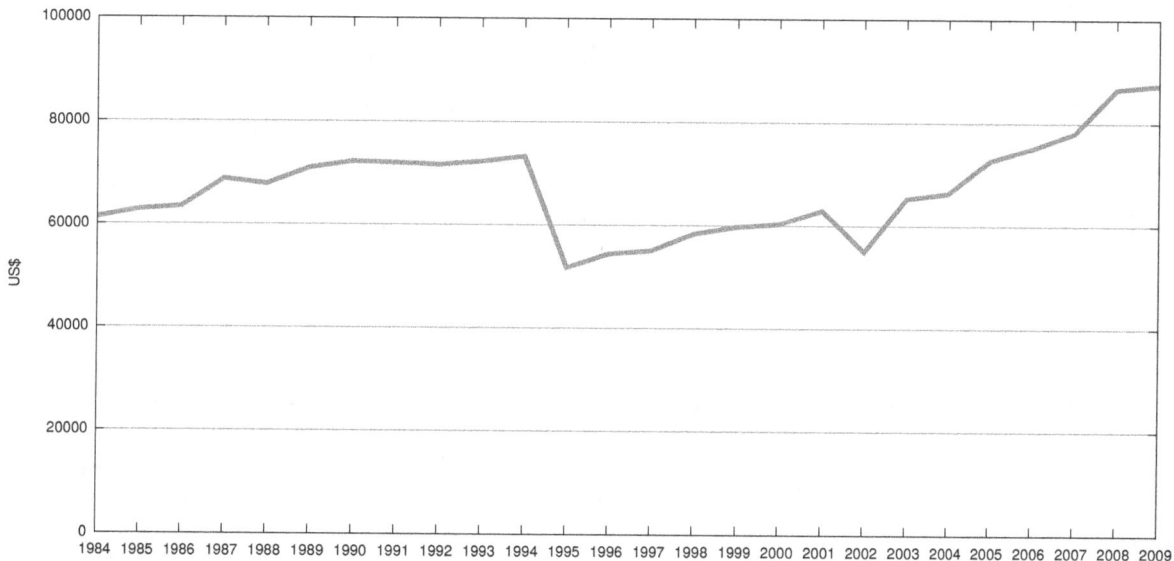

True Cost of Christmas, 1984–2009

The **Christmas Price Index** is a tongue-in-cheek economic indicator, maintained by the U.S. bank PNC Wealth Management, which tracks the cost of the items in the carol "The Twelve Days of Christmas".[*][5][*][6]

9.1   Origins

The Christmas Price Index was conceived by the bank's chief economist as a humorous commodity price index to measure the changing cost of goods over time. Commodity price indices, as compiled by economics, use a "market basket" of certain goods and then measure the cost of the goods from year to year to gauge inflation in different sectors of the economy.

The Christmas Price Index chose the items in the popular Christmas carol "The Twelve Days of Christmas" as its market basket: a partridge in a pear tree, two turtle doves, three French hens, four calling birds, five gold(en) rings, six geese, seven swans, eight maids, nine dancing ladies, ten leaping lords, eleven pipers, and twelve drummers. According to tradition, the purchasing of the items begins on December 26 and ends on January 6.

9.2 Methodology

PNC compiles both a "Christmas Price Index" and "The True Cost of Christmas." The "Christmas Price Index" is calculated by adding the cost of the items in the song. The "True Cost of Christmas," however, is calculated by buying a partridge in a pear tree on each of the twelve days, buying two turtle doves from the second day onward, for a total of 22 turtle doves, etc., for the complete set of 364 items.[7]

The price of each item is set as follows:[8]

- The pear tree comes from a local Philadelphia nursery.

- The partridge, turtle dove, and French hen prices are determined by the Cincinnati Zoo and Botanical Garden.

- The price of a canary at Petco is used for the calling [*sic*] bird, though the price of a blackbird (colly bird) may reflect the original version of the song.

- Gordon Jewelers sets the cost of the gold rings, though the gold rings of the song may actually refer to ring-necked pheasants.[9]

- The maids are assumed to be unskilled laborers earning the federal minimum wage.

- A Philadelphia dance company provides estimates for the salary of "ladies dancing".

- The Philadelphia Ballet estimates the salary for the "leaping lords".

- The going-rate for drummers and pipers is that of a Pennsylvania musicians' union.

9.3 Results

Like other light hearted economic indicators, such as *The Economist's* Big Mac Index which tracks the price of the Big Mac hamburger in different countries, the Christmas Price Index nevertheless produces results which have meaningful interpretations.[10]<ref name=O'Hara>O' Hara, Jr., F.M.; F.M. O'Hara III (2000). *Handbook of United States Economic and Financial Indicators*. Greenwood Press. p. 328. ISBN 0-313-27450-9.</ref>

In general, the prices in the index have reflected the United States's growing service economy—prices for goods have mostly fallen, but prices for labor have risen greatly. The cost of hiring ladies and lords, for example, has risen over 300 percent. After the high cost of the dancers, the seven swans are the most expensive item on the index; the unpredictable breeding cycle of swans makes their supply uncertain.[11] Much as the United States Consumer Price Index excludes volatile energy and food prices from its "core" index, the core Christmas Price Index excludes the swans; for 2008, the total price index rose 8.1% from 2007, while the core index rose only 1.1%.[12] The cheapest item in the index is the partridge, which, in 2008, could be purchased for $20.[12] Costs have generally risen and fallen along with the standard Consumer Price Index.

The survey also tracks the cost of ordering the items online; doing so is significantly more expensive, in part due to shipping costs.[8] In 2008, PNC estimated the total cost at $31,956.62, up 2.3% from 2007, while purchasing all 364 items online would cost $131,150.76, an increase of 1.8%.[12] However, if the buyer were to purchase each item from the least-expensive vendor, the total index would be $19,844.95, a discount of 5.86%.[12]

9.4 Criticisms

The Christmas Price Index has been criticized for a number of reasons.[13] First, the index does not clearly define the products that comprise each of the twelve gifts. For example, the price for the eight "maids-a-milking" only includes the cost of eight laborers at Federal minimum wage, while milking also requires at least a milk cow, which is an additional cost.

Second, the index also relies on only one data source per gift when a more reliable approach might use several retailers.

Third, the index prices products that do not actually correspond with the actual gift described. The ten "lords-a-leaping" are valued by using the cost of hiring male ballet dancers instead of real lords.

9.5   References

[1]   "12 Days of Christmas total cost now tops $107,000". *cfnews13.com*. Retrieved 5 November 2015.

[2]   "PNC's Twelve Days of Christmas Price Index for 2013". *Bloomberg*.

[3]   "PNC Christmas Price Index: Bah, Humbug! PNC Christmas Price Index Surges 7.7 Percent In 2013; Prices Would Cause Ebenezer Scrooge To Cringe" (PDF). PNC Financial Services. 2013-12-02. Retrieved 2013-12-16.

[4]   "Here's The True Cost Of Christmas". *BusinessInsider*.

[5]   Spinner, Jackie (December 20, 2007). "Two Turtledoves, My Love; But Maids-a-Milking? Gone. Whole List? Money Doesn't Grow on Pear Trees". *The Washington Post*. Retrieved 2007-12-20.

[6]   Olson, Elizabeth (2007-12-20). "The '12 Days' Index Shows a Record Increase". *The New York Times*.

[7]   Gaffen, David (January 5, 2007). "That's One Expensive Song". *Marketbeast* (The Wall Street Journal). Retrieved 2007-12-20.

[8]   "PNC Christmas Price Index; History/FAQ". *pncchristmaspriceindex.com*. Archived from the original on 2007-12-29. Retrieved 2007-12-20.

[9]   "The Twelve Days of Christmas". Retrieved 2011-09-08.

[10] Nephin, Dan (November 26, 2007). "'Twelve Days of Christmas' Gets Costly". *Associated Press via Google*. Retrieved 2007-12-20.

[11] Olson, Elizabeth (December 23, 2006). "Those Leaping Lords Don't Come Cheap". *The New York Times*. Retrieved 2007-12-20.

[12] "PNC Christmas Price Index-2008" (PDF). Retrieved 2008-12-17.

[13] http://www.fulcrum.com/12Days_Christmas.htm

9.6   External links

- PNC Christmas Price Index Web site

Chapter 10

Cyber Black Friday

Cyber Black Friday is a marketing term for the online version of Black Friday,[1] the Friday following Thanksgiving Day in the United States. The term made its debut in a 2009 press release entitled "Black Friday Goes Online for Cyber Black Friday".[2] According to the National Retail Federation Black Friday shopping survey, 195 million shoppers visited stores and websites over Black Friday weekend in 2009, up from 172 million last year. One-fourth of Americans shopping over the Black Friday weekend (28.5% or 49 million) were shopping online.[3] comScore reported that Black Friday (November 27, 2009) saw $595 million in online sales, representing an 11% increase versus Black Friday 2008. Gian Fulgoni of comScore said, "Black Friday, better known as a shopping bonanza in brick-and-mortar retail stores, is increasingly becoming one of the landmark days in the online holiday shopping world." [4] Some Cyber Black Friday sales are short-lived, last through the weekend, into Cyber Monday, and beyond.[5]

10.1 Origin of the term

'Cyber Black Friday' was created in 2009 by eCoupons.com after observing that online retailers launched their holiday sales before Cyber Monday to compete with the Black Friday brick and mortar frenzy. According to Talya Schaeffer, founder of Cyber Black Friday, "Cyber Black Friday sales are typically the largest of the season. Online retailers are hoping that by offering early discounts, consumers will shop early and often." [6]

10.2 Black Friday Online Sales

In 2009, most major retailers began Black Friday-style sales online, betting that many would rather click for deals on Thanksgiving or Black Friday than wake up before dawn and head to stores in search of door-busters the following day. Dozens of retailers dangled special offers on their Web sites, though not all were identical to what could be found on Black Friday in stores.[7] On July 23, 2010, Target.com announced its first ever "Back in Black Friday" one-day online-only sale.[8] On October 27, 2010, Sears debuted its "Black Friday Now" campaign with a Black Friday sale on October 30 and 31 and every subsequent Friday until Christmas. Like other retailers, Sears started its Black Friday sale early because consumers were looking to shop earlier in the season and spread out spending in the weeks before Christmas.[9]

10.3 Canada

Because of the strong Canadian dollar, in 2009 Canadian retailers began offering Black Friday sales to keep shoppers on their side of the border.[10] TheSource.ca, Apple.ca and Newegg.ca offered Black Friday online sales.[11]

10.4   United Kingdom

In 2010, Amazon.co.uk offered Cyber Black Friday deals from November 22–26. Amazon.co.uk offered Take That's Progress and Susan Boyle's The Gift CDs for £1 (both albums usually retail at £8.93). "The demand for the albums was incredible," said Brian McBride, managing director of Amazon.co.uk ltd. "Customers were online and ready for the start of 'Black Friday Deals Week', snapping up the thousands of albums that were available at just £1 in a matter of seconds." *[12]

According to Amazon.co.uk, "Although it was originally a US phenomenon, UK retailers are also starting to get in on the act, so hopefully you will grab a bargain or two this year, in the Black Friday 2011 sales." *[13]

In 2011, the number of retails offering Black Friday deals sharply increased, with retailers such as Apple Inc., Currys, PC World, Comet and even Harrods offering deals, in addition to Amazon.

10.5   References

[1]   "What is Black Friday?". theguardian. November 25, 2011. Retrieved 2011-11-25.

[2]   "Black Friday Goes Online for Cyber Black Friday" . CyberBlackFriday.com. November 23, 2009. Retrieved 2010-11-01.

[3]   "Black Friday Verdict: As Expected, Number of Shoppers Up, Average Spending Down" . National Retail Federation. November 29, 2009. Retrieved 2010-11-01.

[4]   "Black Friday Boasts $595 Million in U.S. Online Holiday Spending, Up 11 Percent Versus Year Ago" . comScore. November 29, 2009. Retrieved 2010-11-01.

[5]   "Black Friday online deals lure shoppers to make it a cyber Black Friday" . Christian Science Monitor. November 25, 2011. Retrieved 2011-11-25.

[6]   "10 Strategies for Saving Money" . More Magazine. November 2010. Retrieved 2010-11-01.

[7]   "Retailers Shift Discount Focus Online" . The Wall Street Journal. November 27, 2009. Retrieved 2010-11-01.

[8]   "Target.com 'Daily Deals' Offers First-Ever Back in Black Friday One-Day Sale" . Target.com. July 20, 2010. Retrieved 2010-11-01.

[9]   "Sears Black Friday deals begin early October" . WEWS. October 29, 2010. Retrieved 2010-11-01.

[10]   "Black Friday comes to Canada" . Financial Post. November 26, 2009. Retrieved 2010-11-01.

[11]   "Black Friday Is Tomorrow⋯.In Canada Too" . CTV News. November 26, 2009. Retrieved 2010-11-01.

[12]   "Amazon attempts to bring Black Friday discounts to the UK" . Guardian.co.uk. 2010-11-22. Retrieved 2011-08-23.

[13]   "Amazon.co.uk Black Friday Deals Week" . Amazon.co.uk. Retrieved 2011-08-23.

Chapter 11

Cyber Monday

Cyber Monday is a marketing term for the Monday after the Thanksgiving holiday in the United States. The term "Cyber Monday" was created by marketing companies to persuade people to shop online. The term was coined by Ellen Davis and made its debut on November 28, 2005 in a Shop.org press release entitled "'Cyber Monday Quickly Becoming One of the Biggest Online Shopping Days of the Year" .*[2]

According to the Shop.org/Bizrate Research 2005 eHoliday Mood Study, "77 percent of online retailers said that their sales increased substantially on the Monday after Thanksgiving, a trend that is driving serious online discounts and promotions on Cyber Monday this year (2005)".

In 2014, Cyber Monday online sales grew to a record $2.68 billion, compared with last year's $2.29 billion. However, the average order value was $124, down slightly from 2013's $128.*[3]

The deals on Cyber Monday are online-only and generally offered by smaller retailers that cannot compete with the big retailers. Black Friday generally offers better deals on technology, with nearly 85% more data storage deals than Cyber Monday. The past Black Fridays saw far more deals for small appliances, cutlery, and kitchen gadgets on average than Cyber Monday. Cyber Monday is larger for fashion retail. On the past two Cyber Mondays, there were an average of 45% more clothing deals than on Black Friday. There were also 50% more shoe deals on Cyber Monday than on Black Friday.*[4]

Cyber Monday has become an international marketing term used by online retailers in Argentina, Canada, Chile, China, Colombia, Denmark, Germany, Ireland, Uganda, Japan, Portugal, Sweden and the United Kingdom.

11.1 Origin of term

The term "Cyber Monday" was coined by Ellen Davis,*[5]*[6] and was first used within the ecommerce community during the 2005 holiday season. According to Scott Silverman, the head of Shop.org, the term was coined based on 2004 research showing "one of the biggest online shopping days of the year" was the Monday after Thanksgiving (12th-biggest day historically). Retailers also noted the biggest period was December 5 through 15 of the previous year.*[7] In late November 2005, *The New York Times* reported: "The name Cyber Monday grew out of the observation that millions of otherwise productive working Americans, fresh off a Thanksgiving weekend of window shopping, were returning to high-speed Internet connections at work Monday and buying what they liked." *[8] The idea for having such a holiday was created by Tony Valado, in 2003 while working at 1800Flowers.com, and coined "White Wednesday" to be the day before Thanksgiving for online retailers.*[9]

11.2 United States

11.2.1 Online spending

In 2006, comScore reported that online spending on Cyber Monday jumped 25% to $608 million,[10] 21% to $733 million in 2007,[11] and 15% to $846 million in 2008.[12]

In 2009, comScore reported that online spending increased 5 percent on Cyber Monday to $887 million and that more than half of dollars spent online at US Web sites originated from work computers (52.7 percent), representing a gain of 2.3 percentage points from last year.[13] Buying from home comprised the majority of the remaining share (41.6 percent) while buying from international locations accounted for 5.8 percent. According to comScore chairman Gian Fulgoni, "comScore data have shown that Cyber Monday online sales have always been driven by considerable buying activity from work locations. That pattern hasn't changed. After returning from the long Thanksgiving weekend with a lot of holiday shopping still ahead of them, many consumers tend to continue their holiday shopping from work. Whether to take advantage of the extensive Cyber Monday deals offered by retailers or to buy gifts away from the prying eyes of family members, this day has become an annual ritual for America's online holiday shoppers." [13]

In 2010, comScore reported the first-ever $1 billion online shopping day ($1028M), an increase of 16 percent over 2009.[14] In 2011, comScore reported that Cyber Week saw US consumers spend over $6 billion online from November 28 to December 2.[15] In 2012, comScore reported that Cyber Monday saw a 17% increase in sales from 2011, totaling $1.465 billion.[16] In 2013, Cyber Monday sales continued their growth and recorded their highest grossing day ever at $2.29 billion.

In 2014, the average planned expenditure is $361 per person. 46 percent people expect to pay with credit cards and 43 percent expect to pay with debit cards.[17] Sales are up 8.1% as of 6 p.m. ET, according to IBM Digital Analytics. The average order is $131.66, flat with last year, though the number of transactions is up and people are buying more items on average per order.[18]

11.2.2 Employers and online shopping

U.S. employers have been cracking down on employees using company equipment and company time for non-work-related purposes, including Cyber Monday. As of November 2011, 22% of employers had fired an employee for using the Internet for non-work related activity; 7% of human resource managers surveyed had fired an employee for holiday shopping; and 54% of employers were blocking employees from accessing certain websites.[19][20]

11.3 Other countries

11.3.1 Americas

Argentina

According to Argentine press, Cyber Monday was celebrated on November 11, 2014, and marked a tenfold growth in users taking advantage of online sales over the previous year.[21]

Canada

Cyber Monday came to Canada in 2008.[22] The *National Post* featured an article, in the November 25, 2010, edition, stating that the parity of the Canadian dollar with the US dollar caused many Canadian retailers to have Black Friday and Cyber Monday sales of their own. According to the article, an estimated 80% of Canadians were expected to participate in Black Friday and Cyber Monday sales.[23] Speculation has been made that with all major US television broadcasters —which are typically available to Canadians—emphasizing Black Friday and Cyber Monday sales for stores that are also doing business in Canada, Canadian retailers needed to mimic sales offerings in order to keep Canadian dollars from being spent in the US.[23]

By 2011, around 80% of online retailers in Canada were participating in Cyber Monday.[22]

Chile

Chile's first Cyber Monday took place on 28 November 2011. The companies participating in the event are participants in the Santiago Chamber of Commerce's Electronic Commerce Committee.[*][24]

Colombia

The first Cyber Monday in Colombia took place on 26 November 2012. It was organized by the Colombian Chamber of Electronic Commerce and sponsored by the Ministry of IT and Telecommunications.[*][25]

11.3.2 Asia

India

See also: E-commerce in India

India got its own version of the Cyber Monday (Great Online Shopping Festival) on 12 December 2012 when Google India partnered with many e-commerce companies including Flipkart, Snapdeal, HomeShop18, Indiatimes shopping, and MakeMyTrip. Google said that this was the first time an industry-wide initiative of this scale was undertaken.[*][26]

Japan

Amazon.co.jp announced it registered as Cyber Monday with Japan Anniversary Association in 2012. Amazon.co.jp ran the Cyber Monday Seven Day Sale from Dec 10 through Dec 16, 2012.[*][27]

11.3.3 Europe

France

Inspired by the U.S. phenomenon, the term Cyber Monday was first used in France in 2008.[*][28]

Germany

Amazon.de announced that it brought Cyber Monday to Germany in 2010.[*][29] As of 2014, amazon.de continues to advertise Cyber Monday and has extended it to an 8-day period ("Cyber Monday week") beginning on the Monday before Thanksgiving.

Portugal

In Portugal, the term Cyber Monday was first used in 2009.[*][30]

Sweden

In Sweden Cyber Monday is growing rapidly and several of the largest online retailers regularly launch Cyber Monday campaigns.[*][31] Cyber Monday was first established on larger online retailers in Sweden 2010.[*][32]

United Kingdom

According to a 2009 *The Guardian* article, UK online retailers are now referring to "Cyber Monday" as the busiest internet shopping day of the year that commonly falls on the same day as the US Cyber Monday.*[33]

11.3.4   Middle East

Iran

e-commerce development center of Iran ran the 2nd e-Shop Festival before beginning of new year at 1394 Hijri. Presidential of e-commerce development center in latest Congress of Industrial Management of Iran (23 Feb 2015), announced this year, festival held according to Cyber Monday *[2] concept. More than one thousand ecommerce companies took part in the nationwide advertised event which turned out to be a major success for Iran's ecommerce industry.

11.3.5   Oceania

Australia

Beginning at 7pm AEDT on 20 November 2012, Australian online retailers held a similar event for the first time, dubbed "Click Frenzy". Many websites immediately crashed, went offline, or had major server issues, including the Click Frenzy promotion website. A major Australian retailer, David Jones, ran a competing sale dubbed 'Christmas Frenzy' on the same date.

New Zealand

Online retailer Belly Beyond held the first Cyber Monday Sale in New Zealand on 29 November 2010.*[34] The sale lasted for five days, from Monday to Friday.

11.4   See also

- Green Monday

- Black Friday (shopping)

- Super Saturday (Panic Saturday)

- Giving Tuesday

- Miracle Monday

- Singles Day

11.5   References

[1] "'Cyber Monday in Egypt' Cyber Monday Egypt". *Jumia.com.eg*.

[2] "'Cyber Monday' Quickly Becoming One of the Biggest Online Shopping Days of the Year". *Shop.org*.

[3] http://www.fundivo.com/stats/cyber-monday-statistics/

[4] "What's the difference between Black Friday and Cyber Monday?". *Mirror.co.uk*. Mirror.co.uk. Nov 28, 2013. Retrieved 2014-11-25.

[5] Tschorn, Adam (18 November 2007). "Cyber Monday? Not so much". *Los Angeles Times*. Retrieved 20 May 2015.

[6] Sutter, John D. (29 November 2010). "Why 'Cyber Monday' is mostly myth". *CNN*. Retrieved 20 May 2015.

[7] "Shop 'til your mouse breaks: Etailers await "Cyber" Monday". CNN.com. November 28, 2005. Retrieved November 26, 2007.

[8] Michael Barbaro (November 11, 2005). "Online sales take off on 'Cyber Monday'". *The New York Times*.

[9] "Yahoo! Groups".

[10] "Cyber Monday E-Commerce Spending Beats Forecast; Climbs 25 Percent Versus Last Year to $608 Million". *comScore*. November 2006.

[11] "Cyber Monday Spending Propels Holiday E-Commerce to Strong Week of More than $4 Billion in Sales". *comScore*. December 2007.

[12] "E-Commerce Spending Jumps 15 Percent on Cyber Monday to $846 Million, the Second Heaviest Online Spending Day on Record". *comScore*. December 2008.

[13] "Cyber Monday Online Sales Up 5 Percent vs. Year Ago to $887 Million to Match Heaviest Online Spending Day in History". *comScore*. December 2009.

[14] Anderson, Mae (December 1, 2010). "Cyber Monday biggest spending day online ever, firm says sales top $1 billion". *Chicago Tribune*. Retrieved December 2, 2010.

[15] "'Cyber Week' Results in Record Online Spending of $6 Billion". *WBNG*. December 6, 2011.

[16] "Cyber Monday Prediction Results for 2012". *BestCyberWeek.com*. August 2013.

[17] Menton, Jessica (November 19, 2014). "Most Americans Won't Shop On Black Friday Or Cyber Monday". *Investing.com*. Retrieved November 19, 2014.

[18] De Dios, Princess Eilaine. "Cyber Monday sales trend higher". Retrieved 2 December 2014.

[19] "Shopping On The Clock: Cyber Monday In The Workplace". *aol.com*. Retrieved November 27, 2011.

[20] "Staying Safe Online On Cyber Monday". *http://www.cybermondaysniper.com/*.

[21] "Cyber Monday: creció 10 veces la cantidad de compradores". *Clarín.com* (in Spanish). November 11, 2014. Retrieved November 12, 2014.

[22] Canadian retailers fight back against Black Friday deals, Toronto Start 2012

[23] "Arts". National Post. November 25, 2010 .

[24] "Chile tendra su primer cyber Monday con ineditas ofertas en linea" (in Spanish). La segunda. November 2011

[25] "Celebre el primer cyberlunes oficial en Colombia" (in Spanish). November 25, 2012

[26] "Google partners e-commerce sites for 'Cyber Monday' on December 12". *Economic Times*. December 4, 2012. Retrieved December 31, 2012.

[27] "Amazon.co.jp registered Cyber Monday with Japan Anniversary Association" (in Japanese). JP. Retrieved December 1, 2012.

[28] "Le 24 novembre, le Cybermonday débarque en France". *ZDNet* (in French) (France). Retrieved August 24, 2010.

[29] "Amazon.de bringt Cyber Monday nach Deutschland". *Presseportal* (in German) (DE). Retrieved November 3, 2011.

[30] "Lojas online fazem uma semana de descontos loucos". *Jornal i* (in Portuguese) (PT). Retrieved November 18, 2010.

[31] "Näthandlarnas Cyber Monday slog nya rekord". *Ehandel.se*. Ehandel.se. 2013-12-04. Retrieved 2014-11-25.

[32] "Näthandlarnas Cyber Monday slog nya rekord". *ehandel.se*. ehandel.se. 2013-12-04. Retrieved 2014-11-25.

[33] Teather, David (November 23, 2009). "Amazon gets set for cyber Monday as Christmas shopping online clicks —Internet retailers are preparing for a deluge of online orders on their busiest day of the year in the lead-up to Christmas". London: The Guardian. Retrieved November 23, 2009.

[34] "The Accidentally-on-Purpose History of Cyber Monday". *Esquire*. Retrieved November 29, 2010.

Chapter 12

Economics of Christmas

"Christmas shopping" redirects here. For the album by Buck Owens, see Christmas Shopping (album).

The **economics of Christmas** is significant because Christmas is typically a peak selling season for retailers in many

Christmas market in Jena, Germany

nations around the world. Sales increase dramatically as people purchase gifts, decorations, and supplies to celebrate. In the U.S., the "Christmas shopping season" starts as early as October.[*][1][*][2] In Canada, merchants begin advertising campaigns just before Halloween (October 31), and step up their marketing following Remembrance Day on November 11. In the UK and Ireland, the Christmas shopping season starts from mid November, around the time when high street Christmas lights are turned on.[*][3][*][4] In the United States, it has been calculated that a quarter of all personal spending takes place during the Christmas/holiday shopping season.[*][5] Figures from the U.S. Census Bureau reveal that expenditure in department stores nationwide rose from $20.8 billion in November 2004 to $31.9 billion in December

2004, an increase of 54 percent. In other sectors, the pre-Christmas increase in spending was even greater, there being a November–December buying surge of 100 percent in bookstores and 170 percent in jewelry stores. In the same year employment in American retail stores rose from 1.6 million to 1.8 million in the two months leading up to Christmas.[6] Industries completely dependent on Christmas include Christmas cards, of which 1.9 billion are sent in the United States each year, and live Christmas Trees, of which 20.8 million were cut in the U.S. in 2002.[7] In the UK in 2010, up to £8 billion was expected to be spent online at Christmas, approximately a quarter of total retail festive sales.[4]

During the 2014 holiday shopping season, retail sales in the United States are forecast to increase to a total of over $616 billion, up from 2013's $602 billion. The average US holiday shopper is expected to spend over $800, of which close to 73 percent will be in gifts.[8]

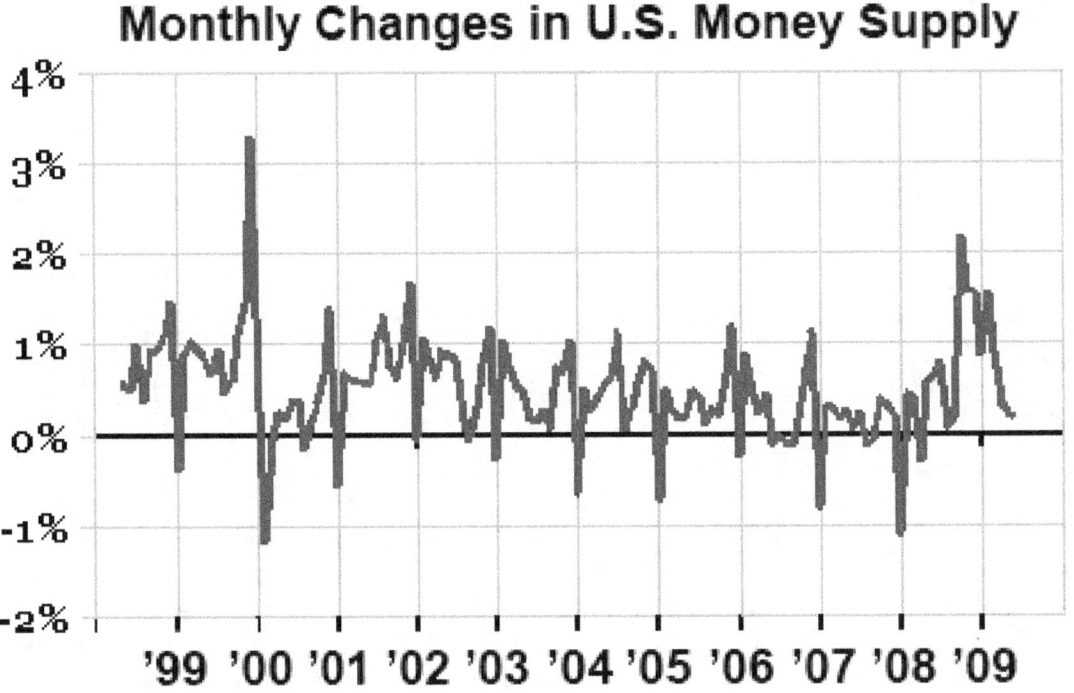

Each year (most notably 2000) money supply in US banks is increased for Christmas shopping.

In most Western nations, Christmas Day is the least active day of the year for business and commerce; almost all retail, commercial and institutional businesses are closed, and almost all industries cease activity (more than any other day of the year), whether laws require such or not. In England and Wales, the Christmas Day (Trading) Act 2004 prevents all large shops from trading on Christmas Day. Scotland is currently planning similar legislation. Film studios release many high-budget movies during the holiday season, including Christmas films, fantasy movies or high-tone dramas with high production values to hopes of maximizing the chance of nominations for the Academy Awards.

One economist's analysis calculates that, despite increased overall spending, Christmas is a deadweight loss under orthodox microeconomic theory, because of the effect of gift-giving. This loss is calculated as the difference between what the gift giver spent on the item and what the gift receiver would have paid for the item. It is estimated that in 2001, Christmas resulted in a $4 billion deadweight loss in the U.S. alone.[9][10] Because of complicating factors, this analysis is sometimes used to discuss possible flaws in current microeconomic theory. Other deadweight losses include the effects of Christmas on the environment and the fact that material gifts are often perceived as white elephants, imposing cost for upkeep and storage and contributing to clutter.[11]

12.1 Preparation

12.1.1 Christmas club

Main article: Christmas club

Christmas clubs are savings programs, the first of which were offered by various banks in the United States during the Great Depression. The concept is that bank customers deposit a set amount of money each week into a special savings account, and receive the money back at the end of the year for Christmas shopping. For decades, financial institutions competed for the holiday savings business, offering enticing premiums and advertising items such as tokens. The Dime Saving Bank of Toledo, Ohio, issued a brass token "good for 25 cents in opening a Christmas account" for 1922-1923. There were also numbered tokens issued by the Atlantic Country Trust Co. in Atlantic City, New Jersey, inscribed on the reverse: "Join our Christmas Club and Have Money When You Need It Most." In the February 2006 issue of *Forbes* magazine, business writer James Surowiecki summarized the accounts' appeal: "The popularity of Christmas club accounts isn't a mystery; if their money was in a regular account, people assumed they'd spend it." [12]

12.1.2 *Sears Wish Book*

Main article: Sears Wish Book

The *Sears Wish Book* is a popular Christmas-gift catalog released by Sears Holdings Corporation, annually in September. The catalog contains toys and other holiday-related merchandise. The first *Sears Wish Book* was printed in 1933, [13] and was a separate big-book catalog from the annual Sears Christmas catalog. In the 2007 edition of the catalog, half of the total number of pages was devoted to Christmas toys and the remainder focused on other store items including appliances, tools, clothes and jewelry. [14]

12.2 Commencement

12.2.1 Christmas creep

Main article: Christmas creep

Christmas creep is a merchandising phenomenon in which merchants and retailers exploit the commercialized status of Christmas by moving up the start of the holiday shopping season.[15] The term was first used in the mid-1980s.[16] It is associated with a desire of merchants to take advantage of particularly heavy Christmas-related shopping well before Black Friday in the United States and before Halloween in Canada. The term is not used in the UK and Ireland, where retailers call Christmas the "golden quarter", that is, the three months of October through December is the quarter of the year in which the retail industry hopes to make the most profit.[17] It can apply for other holidays as well, notably Valentine's Day, Easter and Mother's Day. The motivation for holiday creep is for retailers to lengthen their selling interval for seasonal merchandise in order to maximize profit and to give early-bird shoppers a head start on that holiday. However, it is not clear that this practice has been consistently beneficial for retailers.[18]

12.2.2 United States

Main article: Black Friday (shopping)

Black Friday is the Friday following Thanksgiving Day in the United States (the fourth Thursday of November), often regarded as the beginning of the Christmas shopping season. In recent years, most major retailers have opened extremely early (increasingly even on the night of Thanksgiving itself, albeit not without controversy[19]) and offered promotional sales to kick off the holiday shopping season, similar to Boxing Day sales in many Commonwealth nations. Black Friday is not a holiday, but California and some other states observe "The Day After Thanksgiving" as a holiday for state government employees, sometimes in lieu of another federal holiday such as Columbus Day.[20] Many non-retail employees and schools have both Thanksgiving and the day after off, followed by a weekend, thereby increasing the number of potential

DC USA shopping center on Black Friday

shoppers. It has routinely been the busiest shopping day of the year since 2005,*[21] although news reports, which at that time were inaccurate,*[22] have described it as the busiest shopping day of the year for a much longer period of time.*[23]

12.2.3 Mexico

Main article: El Buen Fin

El Buen Fin is an annual nationwide shopping event in Mexico, in existence since 2011 and taking place on the third weekend of November in Mexico, and the beginning of the Christmas shopping season. On this weekend, major retailers extend their store hours*[24] and offer special promotions, including extended credit terms and price promotions. The purpose of this weekend is to revive the economy by encouraging consumption*[25] and improve the quality of life of all Mexican families by implementing promotions and discounts in the prices of various products. It was inspired by the American celebration, *Black Friday* and emerged as an initiative of Council of Business Coordination,*[26] in association with the federal government and private sector organizations.

12.3 Duration

12.3.1 Christmas market

Main article: Christmas market
  A Christmas market is a street market associated with the celebration of Christmas during the four weeks of Advent.

Christmas market in Jena, Germany

These markets originated in Germany, Austria, South Tyrol, North Italy and many French regions such as Alsace, Lorraine, Savoy,[27] but are now being held in many other countries. The history of Christmas markets goes back to the Late Middle Ages in the German-speaking part of Europe and in many parts of the former Holy Roman Empire that includes many eastern region of France and Switzerland. Dresden's Strietzelmarkt was first held in 1434. The Christmas markets of Bautzen (first held in 1384),[28] Frankfurt (first mentioned in 1393) and Munich (1310) were even older. The Vienna "December market" was a kind of forerunner of the Christmas market and dates back to 1294.

12.3.2 Christmas Price Index

Main article: Christmas Price Index

The Christmas Price Index is a tongue-in-cheek economic indicator, maintained by the U.S. bank PNC Wealth Management, which tracks the cost of the items in the carol "The Twelve Days of Christmas".[29][30] PNC compiles both a "Christmas Price Index" and "The True Cost of Christmas." The "Christmas Price Index" is calculated by adding the cost of the items in the song. The "True Cost of Christmas," however, is calculated by buying a partridge in a pear tree on each of the twelve days, buying two turtle doves from the second day onward, for a total of 22 turtle doves, etc., for the complete set of 364 items.[31]

12.4 Conclusion

12.4.1 United States

Main article: Super Saturday

Super Saturday is the last Saturday before Christmas, a major day of revenue for American retailers, marking the end of the shopping season they and many customers believe begins on Black Friday. Super Saturday targets last-minute shoppers. Typically the day is ridden with one-day sales in an effort to accrue more revenue than any other day in the Christmas and holiday season.[*][32]

12.5 Christmas Day

12.5.1 Christmas Day (Trading) Act 2004

Main article: Christmas Day (Trading) Act 2004

The Christmas Day (Trading) Act 2004 (c 26) is an Act of the Parliament of the United Kingdom. It prevents shops over 280 m²/3,000 sq ft from opening on Christmas Day in England and Wales. Shops smaller than the limit are not affected. The Act was introduced to the House of Commons by Kevan Jones, MP for North Durham as a Private Member's Bill on 7 January 2004. The aim of the Act was to keep Christmas Day a "special" day, whereby all major retailers would be closed. Although it was traditional for major retailers to close on 25 December, some retailers, such as Woolworths, began to open some stores in the late 1990s. Both religious groups and shop worker unions were against the idea of Christmas openings, leading to pressure on the Government to pass legislation to prevent the practice. In 2006, the Scottish Parliament debated a similar law that would apply to shops in Scotland. The law was enacted in 2007 and it contained special provisions for New Year's Day retail activities too.[*][33]

12.6 Criticism

12.6.1 Buy Nothing Christmas

Main article: Buy Nothing Christmas

Buy Nothing Christmas is an ongoing protest and reaction to the commercialization of the North American Christmas season. It started unofficially in 1968, when Ellie Clark and her family decided to publicly disregard the commercial aspects of the Christmas holiday.[*][34] Contemporarily a movement was created to extend Adbusters' Buy Nothing Day into the entire Christmas season.[*][34] Buy Nothing Christmas first became official in 2001 when a small group of Canadian Mennonites created a website and gave the movement a name.[*][35]

12.6.2 Buy Nothing Day

Main article: Buy Nothing Day

Buy Nothing Day is an international day of protest against consumerism. In North America, Buy Nothing Day is held the Friday after U.S. Thanksgiving (November 28, 2014; November 27, 2015; November 25, 2016; November 24, 2017); elsewhere, it is held the following day, which is the last Saturday in November.[*][36][*][37] Buy Nothing Day was founded in Vancouver by artist Ted Dave[*][38] and subsequently promoted by *Adbusters* magazine,[*][39] based in Canada. The first Buy Nothing Day was organized in Canada in September 1992 "as a day for society to examine the issue of over-consumption." In 1997, it was moved to the Friday after American Thanksgiving, also called "Black Friday", which is one of the ten busiest shopping days in the United States. In 2000, advertisements by *Adbusters* promoting Buy Nothing Day were denied advertising time by almost all major television networks except for CNN.[*][36]

12.7 References

[1] Varga, Melody. "Black Friday, *About:Retail Industry.*

[2] "Definition Christmas Creep – What is Christmas Creep". Womeninbusiness.about.com. 2010-11-02. Retrieved 2011-02-24.

[3] South Molton and Brook Street Christmas Lights (Tuesday November 16, 2010) *View London.co.uk*

[4] Julia Kollewe Monday (November 29, 2010) West End spree worth £250m marks start of Christmas shopping season *The Guardian*

[5] Gwen Outen (2004-12-03). "ECONOMICS REPORT – Holiday Shopping Season in the U.S.". Voice Of America.

[6] US Census Bureau. "Facts. The Holiday Season" December 19, 2005. (accessed 2009-11-30)

[7] US Census 2005

[8] Retail Holiday Shopping Statistics

[9] "The Deadweight Loss of Christmas", *American Economic Review*, December 1993, **83** (5)

[10] "Is Santa a deadweight loss?" *The Economist* December 20, 2001

[11] Reuters. "Christmas is Damaging the Environment, Report Says" December 16, 2005.

[12] Surowiecki, James. "Bitter Money and Christmas Clubs." Forbes.com. Feb. 14, 2006.

[13] History of the Sears Catalog

[14] Sears Wish Book Makes a Return

[15] Siewers, Alf (November 25, 1987). "He's well-suited to enjoying life of Santa". *Chicago Sun-Times*. Retrieved December 26, 2007. And so does the culture, with a commercializing of himself that Santa deplores even as he has watched the holiday season creep back to Labor Day.

[16] Maxwell, Kerry (September 18, 2006). "Macmillan English Dictionary Word Of The Week Archive – "Christmas creep"". *New Words*. Macmillan Publishers. Retrieved December 26, 2007. The term Christmas creep was first used in the mid-eighties, though gained wider recognition more recently, possibly due to subsequent coinage of the expression mission creep.

[17] Zoe Wood (Tuesday December 21, 2010) Snow chaos raises fears for Christmas dinners minus the trimmings *The Guardian*

[18] "Christmas Creep: The Shopping Season Is Longer, but Is It Better?". *Knowledge@Wharton*. Wharton School of the University of Pennsylvania. March 1, 2006. Retrieved December 27, 2007. ... Wharton marketing scholars and other analysts say an extended Christmas season is something of a mixed bag. It may hold advantages, disadvantages —or even no advantages —for store owners.

[19] Sreenivasan, Hari (November 22, 2012). "How 'Black Friday' Morphed Into 'Gray Thursday'". *PBS*. Retrieved November 23, 2012.

[20] "Pima County in Arizona Replaces Columbus Day with Black Friday". *BestBlackFriday.com*. 2013-09. Check date values in: |date= (help)

[21] International Council of Shopping Centers. "Holiday Watch: Media Guide 2006 Holiday Facts and Figure" (PDF).; Shopper-Trak, Press Release, ShopperTrak Reports Positive Response to Early Holiday Promotions Boosts Projections for 2010 Holiday Season at the Wayback Machine (archived November 29, 2010) (November 16, 2010).

[22] International Council of Shopping Centers. "Daily Sales Comparison Top Ten Holiday Shopping Days (1996–2001)" (PDF).

[23] *E.g.,* Albert R. Karr, "Downtown Firms Aid Transit Systems To Promote Sales and Build Good Will," *Wall St. J.,* p. 6 (November 26, 1982); Associated Press, "Holiday Shoppers Jam U.S. Stores," *The New York Times*, p. 30 (November 28, 1981).

[24] http://www.excelsior.com.mx/node/784759

[25] Deals or Debt? Mexico's Controversial Black Friday Retrieved 26 June 2013

[26] Mexico Introduces its own version of 'Black Friday' – style shopping blitz Retrieved 26 June 2013

[27] http://noel.org

[28] *Bautzen Christmas Market*

[29] Spinner, Jackie (December 20, 2007). "Two Turtledoves, My Love; But Maids-a-Milking? Gone. Whole List? Money Doesn't Grow on Pear Trees". *The Washington Post*. Retrieved 2007-12-20.

[30] Olson, Elizabeth (2007-12-20). "The '12 Days' Index Shows a Record Increase". *The New York Times*.

[31] Gaffen, David (January 5, 2007). "That's One Expensive Song". *Marketbeast* (The Wall Street Journal). Retrieved 2007-12-20.

[32] Nick Natario. "Holiday Shoppers Pack Stores on Super Saturday". WETM TV. Retrieved 16 June 2010.

[33] Christmas Day and New Year's Day Trading (Scotland) Act 2007 Accessed January 21, 2013

[34] http://www.buynothingchristmas.org/about/index.html

[35] Priesnitz, Wendy. "A Buy Nothing Christmas." *Natural Life Magazine*, November/December 2006. Retrieved 27 November 2008.

[36] "Buy Nothing Day"*The Guardian.co.uk*

[37] "Buy Nothing Day"*Adbusters.org*

[38] Crook, Barbara. "Can you say bye to buying 1 day a year?" *The Vancouver Sun*. September 25, 1992.

[39] Click Here to Buy Nothing. Joanna Glasner. *Wired*, Nov 22, 2000.

Chapter 13

El Buen Fin

El Buen Fin (Literally the "*The Good End*" but implying "*The Good Weekend*") is an annual nationwide shopping event in Mexico, in existence since 2011 and taking place on November in the weekend prior to the Monday in which the Mexican Revolution holiday is pushed from its original date of November the 20th, as a result of the measure taken by the government of pushing certain holidays to the Monday of their week in order to avoid the workers and students to make a "larger" weekend (for example, not attending in a Friday after a Thursday holiday, thus making a 4-day weekend). On this weekend, major retailers extend their store hours*[1] and offer special promotions, including extended credit terms and price promotions.

The purpose of this weekend is to revive the economy by encouraging consumption*[2] and improve the quality of life of all Mexican families by implementing promotions and discounts in the prices of various products. It was inspired by the American celebration, *Black Friday* and emerged as an initiative of Council of Business Coordination,*[3] in association with the federal government and private sector organizations.

13.1   History

Mexican President Felipe Calderón stated his belief that this move will cushion Mexican economy from the threats of European and US economic difficulties.*[4]

The event is organized by

- the Bancos de México's Association

- Mexican Internet Association

- National Association of Supermarkets and Departmental Stores (ANTAD)

- Council of Business Coordinator

- Bosses Confederation of the Mexican Republic (COPARMEX)

- Confederation of National Chambers of Trade, Services and Tourism (Concanaco Servytur)

- Confederation of Industrial Chambers of the United States of Mexico (CONCAMIN), and

- Iniciativa México, in coordination with the Mexico's federal government.

Since 2011, retailers have run campaigns marketing *El Buen Fin* to be the best time of the year to buy goods.*[5] Critics say that Mexico's Black Friday deals are not helpful for Mexican consumers causing them to go into unnecessary debt as most of the offers are monthly payment deals, package deals (i.e. buy 2, get 1 free) or store credit deals (get $300 for every $1000 spent, for example) and not real discounts. Others, such as furniture store chain, Famsa, see it as an opportunity to attract North American buyers, especially in the border cities such as Tijuana, Ciudad Juárez or Reynosa, as *El Buen Fin* is scheduled to be about 1 or 2 weeks before the US Black Friday.

Mexican civil society consumer rights watchdog *El Poder del Consumidor* has said that this economic activity has pushed more Mexicans to credit card debts.[*][6]

13.1.1 Name

In Spanish *El Buen Fin* directly translates as "The Good End", however, this is a short form of *El Buen Fin de Semana*, which translates as "The Good End of the Week".

In Mexico, the expression for "the weekend" is shortened to just "the end" in many informal situations.

13.2 References

[1] http://www.excelsior.com.mx/node/784759

[2] Deals or Debt? Mexico's Controversial Black Friday Retrieved 26 June 2013

[3] Mexico Introduces its own version of 'Black Friday' – style shopping blitz Retrieved 26 June 2013

[4] Economic Stimulus for Mexico, "El Buen Fin": Mexico's Black Friday Retrieved 26 June 2013

[5] Mexico gears up for the first Black Friday-style sales Retrieved 26 June 2013

[6] "Good order" only benefits companies, consumer alert Power Retrieved 26 June 2013

13.3 External links

- [El Ponder del Consumidor membership to the International Consumer Organizations http://www.consumersinternational.org/our-members/member-directory/El%20Poder%20del%20Consumidor%20-%20Consumer%20Power]

- El Buen Fin 2014 Official site.

Chapter 14

Festivus

This article is about the December holiday. For other uses, see Festivus (disambiguation).

Festivus is both a parody and a secular holiday celebrated on December 23 that serves as an alternative to participating in the pressures and commercialism of the Christmas season. It has been described as "the perfect secular theme for an all-inclusive December gathering".*[1]

Originally a family tradition of scriptwriter Dan O'Keefe, who worked on the American sitcom *Seinfeld*, Festivus entered popular culture after it was made the focus of the 1997 episode "The Strike".*[1]*[2] The holiday's celebration, as it was shown on *Seinfeld*, includes a Festivus dinner, an unadorned aluminum Festivus pole, practices such as the "Airing of Grievances" and "Feats of Strength", and the labeling of easily explainable events as "Festivus miracles".*[3]

The episode refers to it as "a Festivus for the rest of us", referencing its non-commercial aspect. It has also been described both as a "parody holiday festival" and as a form of playful consumer resistance.*[4]

14.1 History

Festivus was conceived by editor and author Daniel O'Keefe and was celebrated by his family as early as 1966. In the original O'Keefe tradition, the holiday would take place in response to family tension, "any time from December to May".*[5] The phrase "A Festivus for the rest of us" also derived from an O'Keefe family event, the death of Daniel O'Keefe's mother.*[5]

In 1982, Daniel O'Keefe wrote a book, *Stolen Lightning: The Social Theory of Magic*, that deals with idiosyncratic ritual and its social significance, a theme relevant to Festivus tradition.*[6]

The word Festivus in this sense was coined by O'Keefe, and according to him the name "just popped into my head".*[1] The English word *festive* derives from Latin "festivus", which in turn derives from festus "joyous; holiday, feast day".*[7]*[8]*[9]

Although the first Festivus took place in February 1966, as a celebration of Daniel O'Keefe's first date with his future wife, Deborah,*[1] it is now celebrated on December 23, as depicted in a *Seinfeld* episode written by O'Keefe's son.*[2]

14.1.1 *Seinfeld*

Festivus was introduced in the *Seinfeld* episode "The Strike", written by Daniel O'Keefe's son Dan O'Keefe. The episode revolves around Cosmo Kramer (Michael Richards) returning to work at H&H Bagels. First, while at Monk's Restaurant, Jerry, George and Elaine discuss George's father's creation of Festivus.*[3] Then Kramer becomes interested in resurrecting the holiday when, at the bagel shop, Frank Costanza (Jerry Stiller) tells him how he created Festivus as an alternative holiday in response to the commercialization of Christmas.*[3]

Frank Costanza's son, George (Jason Alexander), creates donation cards for a fake charity called The Human Fund (with the slogan "Money for People") in lieu of having to give office Christmas presents. When his boss, Mr. Kruger (Daniel von Bargen), questions George about a $20,000 check he gave George to donate to the Human Fund as a corporate donation, George hastily concocts the excuse that he made up the Human Fund because he feared persecution for his beliefs—for not celebrating Christmas, but celebrating Festivus. Attempting to call his bluff, Kruger goes home with George to see Festivus in action.*[3]

Kramer eventually goes back on strike from his bagel-vendor job when his manager tells him he cannot have time off for his new-found holiday. Kramer is then seen on the sidewalk picketing H&H Bagels, carrying a sign reading "Festivus yes! Bagels no!" and chanting to anyone passing the store: "Hey! No bagel, no bagel, no bagel..." *[3]

Finally, at Frank's house in Queens, Jerry, Elaine, Kramer and George gather to celebrate Festivus. George brings Kruger to prove to him that Festivus is real.*[3]

14.2 Customary practices

The holiday, as portrayed in the *Seinfeld* episode,*[1]*[10] includes practices such as the "Airing of Grievances", which occurs during the Festivus meal and in which each person tells everyone else all the ways they have disappointed them over the past year. After the meal, the "Feats of Strength" are performed, involving wrestling the head of the household to the floor, with the holiday ending only if the head of the household is actually pinned.*[3]

14.2.1 Festivus pole

In the episode, the tradition of Festivus begins with an aluminum pole. Frank Costanza cites its "very high strength-to-weight ratio" as appealing. During Festivus, the pole is displayed unadorned. According to Frank, "I find tinsel distracting."

Dan O'Keefe credits fellow *Seinfeld* writer Jeff Schaffer with introducing the concept. The aluminum pole was not part of the original O'Keefe family celebration, which centered around putting a clock in a bag and nailing it to a wall.*[11]

The Festivus pole used in the Seinfeld episode was an eight foot tall, 1.5 inch interior diameter, "Schedule 80" aluminum "speed rail" (scaffolding) that came from a storage location under the audience bleachers.*[12]

14.2.2 Festivus dinner

In "The Strike", a celebratory dinner is shown on the evening of Festivus prior to the Feats of Strength and during the Airing of Grievances. The on-air meal shows Estelle Costanza serving a sliced reddish colored meat-loaf shaped food on a bed of lettuce.*[13] In the episode no alcohol is served at the dinner, but George's boss, Mr. Kruger, drinks from a hip flask.*[3]

The original holiday dinner in the O'Keefe household featured turkey or ham followed by a Pepperidge Farm cake decorated with M&M's, as described in Dan O'Keefe's *The Real Festivus*.*[14]

14.2.3 Airing of Grievances

The celebration of Festivus begins with the "Airing of Grievances", which takes place immediately after the Festivus dinner has been served. It consists of each person lashing out at others and the world about how they have been disappointed in the past year.*[15]

14.2.4 Feats of Strength

The Feats of Strength are the final tradition observed in the celebration of Festivus, celebrated immediately following (or in the case of "The Strike", *during*) the Festivus dinner. The head of the household selects one person at the Festivus

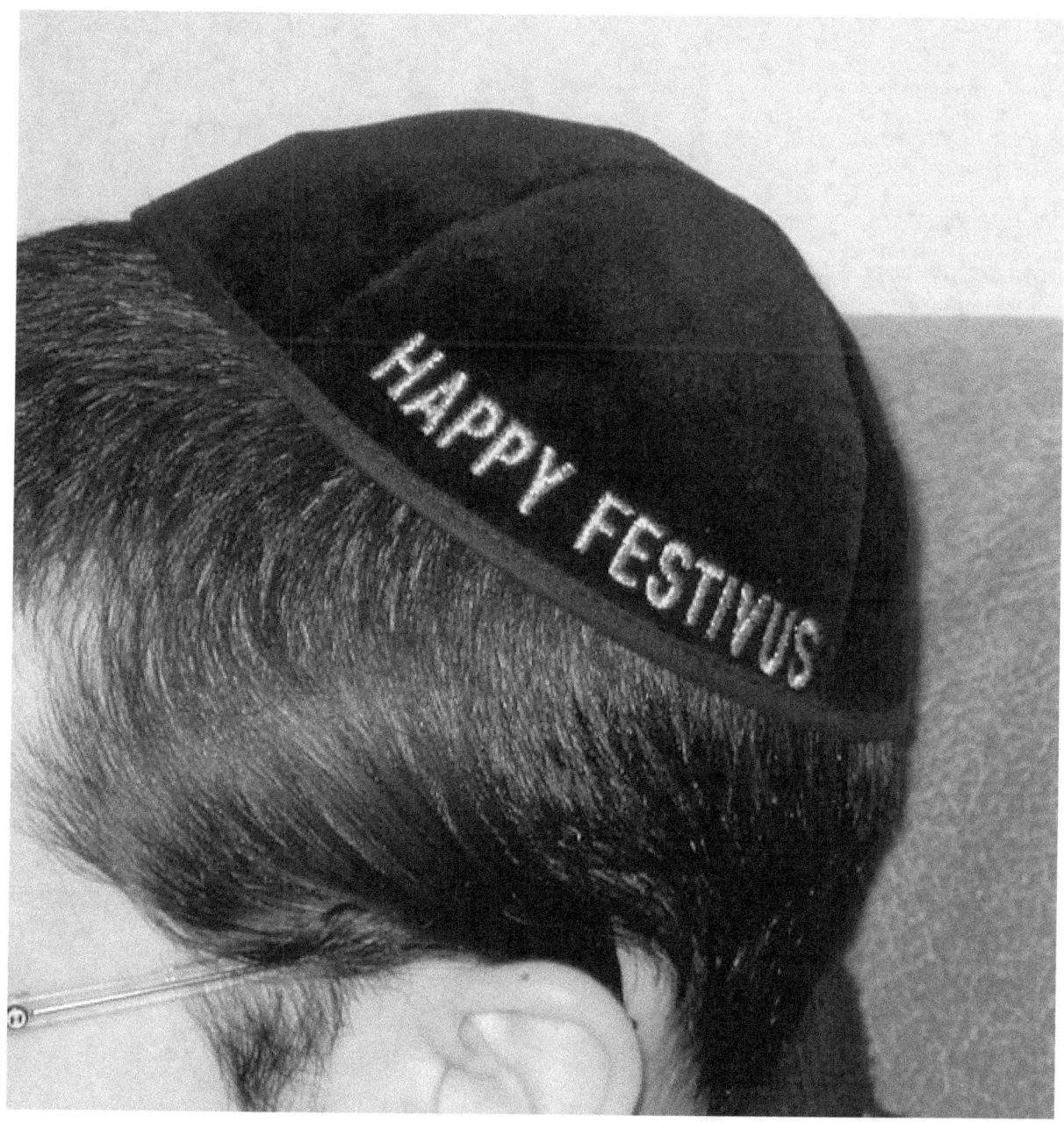

"Happy Festivus" embroidered on a yarmulke.

celebration and challenges them to a wrestling match. Tradition states Festivus is not over until the head of the household is pinned. In "The Strike", however, Kramer manages to circumvent the rule by creating an excuse to leave. The Feats of Strength are mentioned twice in the episode before they actually take place. In both instances, no detail was given as to what had actually happened, but in both instances, George Costanza ran out of the coffee shop in a mad panic, implying he had bad experiences with the Feats of Strength in the past. What the Feats of Strength entailed was revealed at the very end of the episode, when it actually took place. Failing to pin the head of the household results in Festivus continuing until such requirement is met.*[3]

Some Festivus celebrants emulate the colors shown in the Seinfeld series by serving meatloaf placed on a bed of lettuce.

14.2.5 Festivus miracles

Cosmo Kramer twice declares a "Festivus Miracle" during the Festivus celebration in the Costanza household. It is the character Kramer that actually causes the occurrence of two "miracles" by inviting two off-track betting bookies to dinner with Elaine (men whom Elaine wished to avoid), and by causing Jerry's girlfriend Gwen to believe that Jerry was cheating on her.[16] Dan O'Keefe has said "Festivus Miracle" was something his own father used to say, which he actually recalled as writer David Mandel pitched it for the episode. [17]

14.3 Wider adoption

Some people, most of them inspired by the *Seinfeld* episode,[1] subsequently began to celebrate the holiday with varying degrees of seriousness. Allen Salkin's 2005 book *Festivus: The Holiday for the Rest of Us*[5] chronicles the early adoption of Festivus. Rabbi Joshua Eli Plaut's book *A Kosher Christmas: 'Tis the Season to Be Jewish* (Rutgers University Press, 2012) references Festivus, along with hybrid holidays such as Chrismukkah. Released in 2015, *Festivus! The Book: A Complete Guide to the Holiday for the Rest of Us* [17] effectively demonstrates how the holiday continues to be celebrated by people worldwide.

In 2000, Baltimore Ravens head coach Brian Billick would not allow his NFL football team's players to discuss the possibility of competing in that season's Super Bowl. Instead, he and the rest of the Ravens players and staff referred to the NFL playoffs as Festivus, and the Super Bowl as Festivus Maximus. In 2005, Wisconsin Governor Jim Doyle was declared "Governor Festivus" and during the holiday season displayed a Festivus Pole in the family room of the Executive Residence in Madison, Wisconsin.[18] Governor Doyle's 2005 Festivus Pole is now part of the collection of the Wisconsin Historical Museum.[19]

In 2010, a CNN story featuring Jerry Stiller detailed the increasing popularity of the holiday, including US Representative Eric Cantor's Festivus fundraiser,[20] and the *Christian Science Monitor* reported that Festivus was a top trend on Twitter that year.[*][21] In 2012, Google introduced a custom search result for the term "Festivus". In addition to the normal results an unadorned aluminum pole was displayed running down the side of the list of search results and "A Festivus Miracle!" prefixes the results count and speed.[*][22][*][23]

In 2012, a Festivus Pole was erected on city property in Deerfield Beach, Florida, alongside religious themed holiday displays.[*][24] A similar Festivus Pole was displayed next to religious displays in the Wisconsin State Capitol, along with a banner provided by the Freedom From Religion Foundation advocating for the separation of government and religion.[*][25]

In 2013, a Festivus Pole constructed with 6 feet (1.8 m) of beer cans was erected next to a nativity scene and other religious holiday displays in the Florida State Capitol Building.[*][25]

14.4 O'Keefe family practices

The O'Keefe family holiday featured other practices, as detailed in *The Real Festivus* (2005), a book by Daniel O'Keefe's son, Dan O'Keefe.[*][14][*][26] Besides providing a first-person account of the early version of the Festivus holiday as celebrated by the O'Keefe family, the book relates how Dan O'Keefe amended or replaced details of his father's invention to create the *Seinfeld* episode.[*][27]

14.4.1 Festivus Clock

In a 2013 CNN segment on the origins of Festivus, O'Keefe spoke about the real-life experiences related to the holiday. O'Keefe's father, who originated some of the now-recognized Festivus traditions, used a clock, not an aluminum pole. O'Keefe told CNN:

> "The real symbol of the holiday was a clock that my dad put in a bag and nailed to the wall every year...I don't know why, I don't know what it means, he would never tell me. He would always say, 'That's not for you to know.'"[*][28]

14.5 See also

- Buy Nothing Christmas

- Buy Nothing Day

- *What Would Jesus Buy?*, a 2007 documentary

14.6 References

[1] Salkin, Allen (2004-12-19). "Fooey to the World: Festivus Is Come". *The New York Times*. Retrieved 2008-01-09.

[2] "Festivus for the rest of us". *LJWorld*. Retrieved 2006-12-25.

[3] "The Strike". *Seinfeld Scripts*. Retrieved 2012-12-25.

[4] Mikkonen, Ilona; Bajde, Domen (10 April 2012). "Happy Festivus! Parody as playful consumer resistance". *Consumption Markets & Culture* **16** (4): 1–27. doi:10.1080/10253866.2012.662832.

[5] Allen Salkin (2005). *Festivus: The Holiday for the Rest of us*. ISBN 0-446-69674-9.

[6] O'Keefe, Daniel (1982). *Stolen Lightning: A Social Theory of Magic*. ISBN 0-8264-0059-0.

[7] "festus". *Words*. Retrieved 2007-12-27.

[8] "Our day, our way". *Journal Sentinel Online*. Archived from the original on 2006-12-17. Retrieved 2006-12-25.

[9] "Dictionary Entry: Fest-/Festivus", Latin Dictionary and Grammar Aid, University of Notre Dame

[10] Ravitz, Jessica. "Seinfeld' over, but Festivus keeps giving". *CNN.com*. Retrieved 2010-04-09.

[11] "The Origins of Festivus I". cnn.com. 2013-12-24. Retrieved 2013-12-24.

[12] Mark Nelson (2015). *Festivus! The Book*. ISBN 1511556390.

[13] "Festivus Dinner". Festivusweb.com. 1997-12-18. Retrieved 2015-08-19.

[14] O'Keefe, Dan. *The Real Festivus*. Perigee, 2005.

[15] "Happy Festivus I A Festivus for the Rest of Us! I Festivus Feats of Strength, Festivus Airing of Grievances, Festivus Pole". Festivusweb.com. 1997-12-18. Retrieved 2013-07-06.

[16] "Festivus Miracle I Festivusweb.com I Seinfeld Festivus". Festivusweb.com. Retrieved 2013-07-06.

[17] Mark Nelson (2015). *Festivus! The Book*. ISBN 1511556390.

[18] "Gov. Festivus!". *madison.com*. Retrieved 2006-12-25.

[19] "Governor Doyle's Festivus Pole". *Wisconsin Historical Society*. Retrieved 2014-12-21.

[20] "Festivus for the rest of Us! Jerry Stiller on Fake holiday's real popularity". CNN. December 23, 2010. Retrieved 2010-12-23.

[21] "Festivus becomes worldwide holiday. Break out the Festivus pole!". *Christian Science Monitor*. Retrieved 2010-12-23.

[22] Cuts, Matt, (10 December 2012) It's a Festivus miracle when you go to Google and search···, Google+, retrieved 23 December 2013

[23] "Festivus: The Google Easter egg for the rest of us". *National Post*. December 12, 2012. Retrieved 2012-12-13.

[24] Funcheon, Deirdra (2013-12-06). ""Festivus Pole" Made of Beer Cans Approved; Will Go Up in Florida Capitol Next to Jesus' Manger. Deirdra Funcheon. Broward Palm Beach New Times.". Blogs.browardpalmbeach.com. Retrieved 2014-07-20.

[25] Farrington, Brendan (2013-12-11). "Festivus For The Rest Of Us! Florida Atheist Successfully Puts Up Beer Can Pole Display". Huffington Post. Retrieved 2013-12-24.

[26] Dan O'Keefe at the Internet Movie Database

[27] "Origins of Festivus". Retrieved 2015-08-19.

[28] "The Origins of Festivus I". cnn.com. 2013-12-24. Retrieved 2013-12-24.

14.7 External links

- Festivusweb.com - Festivus quotes and the script from "The Strike"

- Origins of Festivus

Chapter 15

Giving Tuesday

Giving Tuesday, often stylized as #GivingTuesday for purposes of hashtag activism, refers to the Tuesday after U.S. Thanksgiving in the United States. It is a movement to create a national day of giving at the beginning of the Christmas and holiday season. Giving Tuesday was started in 2012 by the 92nd Street Y and the United Nations Foundation as a response to commercialization and consumerism in the post-Thanksgiving season (Black Friday and Cyber Monday).[*][1][*][2]

15.1 History

15.1.1 Summary of money moved

15.1.2 2012

The idea for Giving Tuesday was first announced in October 2012, a month before the first planned Giving Tuesday (November 27, 2012). The announcement was made by Giving Tuesday founding partner Mashable, a technology website.[*][1] Other founding partners listed in the story were Skype (launching Skype for Peace) and Cisco. Other partner organizations announced over the coming weeks included Microsoft,[*][8] Sony, Aldo, Case Foundation, Heifer International, Phoenix House, and Starwood Hotels.[*][9] Mashable provided detailed coverage of Giving Tuesday.[*][10][*][11]

Other news and opinion websites that announced Giving Tuesday well in advance were CNet,[*][12] the *Huffington Post*,[*][13] and Deseret News.[*][14]

Shortly before, during, and after the date, Giving Tuesday was covered by *Washington Post*,[*][15] the White House official blog,[*][16] ABC News,[*][17] and the *Huffington Post*.[*][18][*][19] *Forbes* used the occasion to publish a guide to effective giving.[*][20]

15.1.3 2013

Mashable also covered Giving Tuesday in 2013,[*][21] including a partnership with Google+ to hold a "hangout-athon" for Giving Tuesday.[*][22] The *Huffington Post* also covered Giving Tuesday extensively.[*][23]

Giving Tuesday also received coverage in many philanthropy information websites, including Charity Navigator[*][24] and the *Chronicle of Philanthropy*.[*][25][*][26][*][27] The December 4 *Chronicle of Philanthropy* article highlighted a donation by Good Ventures (a foundation funded by Dustin Moskovitz and run by his wife Cari Tuna) to GiveDirectly, Google's hangout-a-thon, and matching grants announced by the Case Foundation.

Giving Tuesday was also covered by mainstream newspapers such as the *Los Angeles Times*[*][28] and *USA Today*.[*][3]

Charitable giving on Giving Tuesday in 2013 was approximately twice the value in 2012.[*][3][*][26][*][27] Over 7,000 nonprofits participated in the 2013 Giving Tuesday.[*][25]

15.1.4   2014

In 2014, the #GivingTuesday movement launched the #GivingTower. The #GivingTower is a partnership between 92nd Street Y, the United Nations Foundation, and Crowdrise. Every donation in the #GivingTower represents a brick in the virtual Tower. [*][29]

Philanthropy News Digest, the *Chronicle of Philanthropy* and *Mashable* reported estimates by the Indiana University Lilly Family School of Philanthropy (with help from the Case Foundation), based on payments processed by Blackbaud, DonorPerfect, GlobalGiving, Network for Good, and Razoo, that a total of $45.7 million was donated on Giving Tuesday ($34.9 million online, and $10.8 million offline that were processed on the next day). [*][5][*][4][*][6][*][7] Of this, $26.1 million was processed by Blackbaud. [*][4] The tally did not include $7.5 million that Indiegogo claimed to have raised for 419 nonprofits on that day. [*][4]

15.2   Reception

Reception of Giving Tuesday has generally been positive, with a large number of organizations, including Google, Microsoft, Skype, Cisco, UNICEF, the Case Foundation, and others joining in as partners. [*][30] Giving Tuesday has been praised as an antidote to consumer culture and as a way for people to give back. [*][14][*][24][*][26]

Timothy Ogden, managing director of the Financial Access Initiative at New York University and board member at effective altruism organization GiveWell, wrote articles for the Stanford Social Innovation Review skeptical of Giving Tuesday, one in 2012[*][31] and another in 2013. [*][32]

15.3   References

[1] Fox, Zoe (October 23, 2012). "6 Inspiring Organizations Joining in #GivingTuesday". Mashable. Retrieved February 15, 2014.

[2] "#GivingTuesday: About". Giving Tuesday. Retrieved February 15, 2014.

[3] Ostendorff, Jon (December 10, 2013). "Growth in online 'Giving Tuesday numbers 'inspiring'". Retrieved February 15, 2014.

[4] Held, Tom (December 4, 2014). "Giving Tuesday Shows Strong Growth in Both Donations and Volunteerism". *Chronicle of Philanthropy*. Retrieved November 1, 2015.

[5] "Third Annual #GivingTuesday Raises $45.7 Million for Charity". *Philanthropy News Digest*. December 5, 2014. Retrieved November 1, 2015.

[6] Herrling, Sheila (December 3, 2014). "#GivingTuesday Moves From Campaign To Tradition". Case Foundation. Retrieved November 1, 2015.

[7] Petronzio, Matt (December 3, 2014). "Giving Tuesday sets record in online donations this year". *Mashable*. Retrieved November 1, 2015.

[8] Fox, Zoe (November 2, 2012). "5 Companies Making Change on #GivingTuesday". Mashable. Retrieved February 15, 2014.

[9] Fox, Zoe (November 20, 2012). "6 Inspiring Companies Joining #GivingTuesday". Mashable. Retrieved February 15, 2014.

[10] Fox, Zoe (November 27, 2012). "10 Ways You Can Take Action for #GivingTuesday". Mashable. Retrieved February 15, 2014.

[11] "Giving Tuesday (category)". Mashable.

[12] Matyszczyk, Chris (November 19, 2012). "Giving Tuesday: Your penance after Black Friday, Cyber Monday: In order to assuage your guilt, crowdfunding platform Razoo wants you to give to charities. Can this possibly catch on?". CNet. Retrieved February 15, 2014.

[13] Case, Jean (November 19, 2012). "Giving Tuesday -- What the Season of Giving Really Means". *Huffington Post*. Retrieved February 15, 2014.

[14] White, Mercedes (November 15, 2012). "Giving Tuesday to give Black Friday a run for its money". *Huffington Post.* Retrieved February 15, 2014.

[15] Gowen, Annie (November 27, 2012). "Organizers launch 'Giving Tuesday' to help charities". *Washington Post.* Retrieved February 15, 2014.

[16] Greenblatt, Jonathan (November 27, 2012). "Giving Tuesday". Retrieved February 15, 2014.

[17] Kim, Susanna (November 26, 2012). "Charities Fight Consumerism With Giving Tuesday". Retrieved February 15, 2014.

[18] Prois, Jessica (November 27, 2012). "Giving Tuesday Offers Worthy Ways To Give". *Huffington Post.* Retrieved February 15, 2014.

[19] "Giving Tuesday Spurred 113% Spike In Number Of Donations". *Huffington Post.* November 30, 2012. Retrieved February 15, 2014.

[20] Mayer, Caroline (November 26, 2012). "Giving Tuesday: 6 Mistakes to Avoid When Giving to Charity". *Forbes.* Retrieved February 15, 2014.

[21] Fox, Zoe (December 3, 2013). "15 Giving Tuesday Campaigns Making a Difference". Mashable. Retrieved February 15, 2014.

[22] Mashable Team (December 2, 2013). "Google+ and Mashable to Host First Hangout-a-thon for Charity". Mashable. Retrieved February 15, 2014.

[23] "Giving Tuesday". Retrieved February 15, 2014.

[24] "#GivingTuesday: A Day of Giving Back". Charity Navigator. October 24, 2013. Retrieved February 15, 2014.

[25] Flandez, Raymund (November 26, 2013). "Giving Tuesday's Second Year Brings More Participation". *Chronicle of Philanthropy.* Retrieved February 15, 2014.

[26] Flandez, Raymund; Frostenson, Sarah (December 4, 2013). "Giving Tuesday Shows Robust Results". *Chronicle of Philanthropy.* Retrieved February 15, 2014.

[27] Flandez, Raymund; Frostenson, Sarah (December 5, 2013). "Giving Tuesday Doubled Donations in 2nd Year". *Chronicle of Philanthropy.* Retrieved February 15, 2014.

[28] White, Ronald (December 2, 2013). "Charities hope to make 'GivingTuesday' as big as Black Friday". *Los Angeles Times.* Retrieved February 15, 2014.

[29] Murray, Elizabeth (November 30, 2014). "Edward Norton on Giving Tuesday". TodayShow. Retrieved December 1, 2014.

[30] "#GivingTuesday: Partners". February 15, 2014.

[31] Ogden, Timothy (November 26, 2012). "The Curmudgeon's Guide to Giving Tuesday: The effort to make giving public and start a "giving season" won't materially affect giving in any positive way.". Stanford Social Innovation Review. Retrieved February 15, 2014.

[32] Ogden, Timothy (December 4, 2013). "What, Exactly, Is Giving Tuesday's Theory of Change? Giving Tuesday seems poised to be a permanent fixture in the philanthropic landscape. So what's the theory of change behind it?". Stanford Social Innovation Review. Retrieved February 15, 2014.

15.4 External links

- Official website

Chapter 16

Green Monday

This article is about the unofficial shopping holiday. For the Eastern Orthodox movable feast, see Clean Monday. For Green Monday in general, see Green Monday (disambiguation).

Green Monday is an online retail industry term similar to Cyber Monday. The term was coined[*][1] by eBay to describe its best sales day in December,[*][2][*][3] usually the second Monday of December. Green Monday is defined more specifically by business research organization comScore as the Monday with at least 10 days prior to Christmas. In 2009, $854 million was spent online in the US on Green Monday,[*][4] with sales in 2011 reaching $1.133 billion.[*][5] In 2012, Green Monday topped out at $1.27 billion, up 13% from 2011 and the third heaviest online sales day for the season behind Cyber Monday and Dec. 4, 2012 (which had no marketing tie-in), according to comScore.[*][6]

In 2014, Green Monday online sales grossed a record $1.6 billion, albeit still lower than Cyber Monday's $2.68 billion during the same year.

16.1 References

[1] "Bargain Hunters Continue Finding Great Deals on eBay This Cyber Monday" (Press release). San Jose, California: eBay. 2 December 2008. Archived from the original on 4 January 2011.

[2] Perez, Juan Carlos (24 December 2007), "ComScore: Last Week Saw Strong Online Shopping", *PC World* (IDG News Service)

[3] "Have you heard of "Green Monday" ?". WHEC. 8 December 2014. Retrieved 8 December 2014.

[4] "Green Tuesday Reaches Record $913 Million in Online Spending", comscore.com, December 2009.

[5] Hargrove, Kelli. "Online Retail Spending up 14% For Q4", *Transworld Business*, 8 February 2012.

[6] TheStreet.com "Bargain Hunters Continue Finding Great Deals on eBay This Cyber Monday" December 2013

Chapter 17

Sears Wish Book

The **Sears Wish Book** is a popular Christmas-gift catalog released by Sears Holdings Corporation, annually in August or September. The catalog contains toys and other holiday-related merchandise. The first *Sears Wish Book* was printed in 1933, [1] and was a separate big-book catalog from the annual Sears Christmas catalog.

17.1   Sears, Roebuck & Co.

In 1993, According to the Los Angeles Times, the Sears catalog offered customers around the US a chance to wear "city clothes" throughout its 97-year-history.[2]

In the same year, Sears discontinued publishing their big-book catalogs in the United States and the Wish Book noticeably started to diminish in size. [3] By 2005, Sears had completely abandoned anything resembling the original Wish Book and was producing the 2.5-by-2.5-inch *Little Big Wish Book* The mini-catalog was given to customers at Sears Auto Centers, placed inside packages that were purchased on Sears.com and Landsend.com, and was included inside the packaging of in-home deliveries.

In 2007, Sears once again created a holiday gift Wish Book'called more reminiscent of its predecessor, however, it was still considerably smaller than the original *Wish Book* at only about 100 pages. This was a stark contrast to the 300-plus page catalog previously produced.[4] According to the Associated Press at that time, the Sears Wish Book was considered as a holiday treat in itself by generations of children who were hoping for the best [5] on Christmas morning.

In the 2007 edition of the catalog, half of the total number of pages was devoted to Christmas toys and the remainder focused on other store items including appliances, tools, clothes and jewelry. [6]

In the 2010 edition, Sears Christmas Wish Book went mobile [7] so customers would be able to access their catalog via smartphone devices.

17.2   Sears Canada

In Canada, Sears continues to distribute their big-book catalogues, including the *Wish Book*.[8] In 2012, Sears Canada chief Calvin McDonald hand-delivered Christmas catalogs [9] to mark the 60th Anniversary of the Sears Wish Book.[10]

Sears Canada launched an iPad app for the 2013 Christmas Wish Book which is currently ranked as the number one free iPad app in Canada in the Catalogue category.[11]

17.3   References

[1]   "History of the Sears Catalog" . *searsarchives.com.*

[2] Mourning the passing of Wish Book Era: Retailing: Sear's Big book was more than a catalogue

[3] "Sears' Wish Book What Does Its Passing Say About Us?". *philly-archives.*

[4] Todé, Chantal (2007-10-03). "New Sears Wish Book a blast from the past". Direct Marketing News.

[5] "Holiday classic: Sears brings back Wish Book". *msnbc.com.*

[6] "Sears Wish Book Makes a Return". *Multichannel Merchant.*

[7] "Sears Wish Book Goes Mobile". *hfnmag.com.*

[8] "Page Not Found". *sears.ca.*

[9] Sears Canada chief hand-delivers Wish Books on old route

[10] "Sears Canada Launches 60th Edition of Its Annual Wish Book". *Reuters.*

[11] Sears Canada launches its updated shoppable iPad application with the Christmas Wish Book

17.4   External links

- Wishbook Web - online scans of pages from several past Wish Books and other Christmas catalogs

- 1982 Sears Christmas Catalog - online scans of pages from 1982 Wish Book

- Sears Canada launches its app with Christmas Wish book

- Online version of Sears Wish Book

Chapter 18

Singles Day

Singles' Day or *Guanggun Jie* (Chinese: 光棍节; pinyin: *Guānggùn Jié*; Wade–Giles: *Kuang-kun chieh*; literally: "bare sticks holiday") is a day for people who are single, celebrated on November 11 (11/11). The date is chosen for the connection between singles and the number '1'. This holiday became popular among young Chinese people.[1] In recognition of the day, young singles organize parties and Karaoke to meet new friends or try their fortunes. It has become the largest online shopping day in the world,[2] with sales in Alibaba's sites Tmall and Taobao at US$5.8 billion in 2013 and US$9.3 billion in 2014.[3]

18.1 Origins

Singles' Day or Bachelors' Day was initially celebrated at various universities in Nanjing during the 1990s, and originated from Nanjing University in 1993. It got the name "Singles' Day" because the date consists of four "one"s. These college students have since graduated, and carried the university tradition into society. Singles' Day has been largely popularized in the internet era and is now observed by youth in several regions outside China as well.

Singles' Day serves as an occasion for single people to party with single friends. The holiday was initially only celebrated by young men, hence the name, "Bachelors' Day," but is now widely celebrated by both genders. 'Blind date' parties are also popular during this day in an attempt to bid goodbye to their single lives. Some schools of a university put forward a special program to gather singles together for celebration. Singles may take on a bemoaning or self-deprecating attitude for remaining single as a university student, but this has helped curb that negativity.

2011 marked the "Singles Day of the Century" (Shiji Guanggun Jie), this date having six "ones" rather than four—an excuse to take celebrations to a higher level.[4] Shopping promotions were highlighted throughout China and activities were widespread. Although this date is meant to celebrate singlehood, the desire to find a spouse or mate is often expressed by young Chinese on this date, and other love-related issues are discussed by the Chinese media.

18.2 Celebration

For breakfast on Singles' Day, singles often eat four Youtiao (deep-fried dough sticks) representing the four "ones" in "11.11" and one Baozi (steamed stuffed bun) representing the middle dot.

In 2011, an above-average number of marital celebrations occurred in Hong Kong and Beijing on November 11.[5] In addition to meaning 'single,' the four 'ones' of the date can also mean 'only one' as in 'the only one for me.' Some people will use this date and this meaning to tell their special someone that they are the only 'one' in their heart.

As more people join in the celebration of this holiday, it has become a great opportunity for companies targeting younger consumers, including restaurants, Karaoke, and online shopping malls. For example, the Chinese online shopping mall Taobao sold 19 billion CNY (about 3 billion USD) of goods on November 11, 2012 [6]

In episode 6 of *The Apprentice (UK Series Four)*, team Alpha made a range of themed greeting cards revolving around National Singles' Day,[7] which garnered mixed reception from buyers *Clinton Cards*, *Celebrations* and *Tesco*. Initially, the team planned to designate February 13—the day before Valentine's Day—National Singles' Day. However, Clinton Cards, and Tesco questioned this decision to designate a competing holiday, considering Valentine's Day is one of the major greeting card seasons. Tesco also questioned the market, asking who would send the cards to the single people.

18.3 Copyrights

The term " 双十一" (meaning "Double 11") was trademarked in China by Alibaba Group on Dec 28, 2012 under registration numbers 10136470 and 10136420. In Oct 2014, Alibaba threatened legal action against media outlets that accept advertising from competitors that use this term.[8]

18.4 See also

- Cyber Monday

- Sheng nu (剩女, shèngnǚ"), so-called "leftover women" who remain unmarried

- Black Friday (shopping)

- Boxing Day

18.5 References

[1] CNN China China's biggest problem? Too many men, November 2012

[2] C. Custer (October 14, 2014). "Tmall CEO: this year, Alibaba plans to take Singles Day global". *Tech in Asia*. Retrieved October 20, 2014.

[3] Steven Millward (November 12, 2014). "New record for world's biggest shopping day as Alibaba's shoppers spend $9.3 billion in 24 hours". *Tech in Asia*. Retrieved December 5, 2014.

[4] A holiday invasion – Why are Chinese enthusiastically adopting new festive events? Thinking Chinese, November 2011

[5] Wall Street Journal (2011). Chinese Couples Rush to the Altar on 11/11/11. Retrieved 16 November 2011.

[6] VB business,online mall Taobao reports $3B in sales in one day, Nov. 2012

[7] Episode 6 Synopsis at BBC Apprentice Microsite

[8] Eric Johnson (Nov 6, 2014). "The Chinese government has essentially given Alibaba the 'Double 11' market". *InvestorPlace*. Retrieved Nov 10, 2014.

18.6 External links

- Creative Singles Day

- A special day for singles

- Home / From Agencies China Focus: Couples rush to marry, singles look for romance on "Super Single's Day"

Chapter 19

Small Business Saturday

Small Business Saturday is an American shopping holiday held on the Saturday after US Thanksgiving during one of the busiest shopping periods of the year.

19.1 History

First observed on November 27, 2010, it is a counterpart to Black Friday and Cyber Monday, which feature big box retail and e-commerce stores respectively. By contrast, Small Business Saturday encourages holiday shoppers to patronize brick and mortar businesses that are small and local. *Small Business Saturday* is a registered trademark of American Express corporation.

In 2010 the holiday was conceived and promoted by American Express via a nationwide radio and television advertising campaign. That year Amex bought advertising inventory on Facebook, which it in turn gave to its small merchant account holders,*[1] and also gave rebates to new customers to promote the event.*[2]*[3]

American Express publicized the initiative using social media, advertising, and public relations. At least 41 local politicians and many small business groups in the United States issued proclamations concerning the campaign,*[4]*[5]*[6] which generated more than one million Facebook "like" registrations and nearly 30,000 tweets under the Twitter hashtags #smallbusinesssaturday (which had existed since early 2010) and #smallbizsaturday.*[7]

19.2 Hashtag

The Twitter hashtag #SmallBusinessSaturday has existed since early 2010 and was used to promote small businesses on any Saturday (not solely that Saturday between Black Friday and Cyber Monday). The hashtag is used in a manner similar to #FollowFriday to highlight favorite local businesses. Additionally, some small business owners have run marketing specials on the November Small Business Saturday to help capitalize on the boost in foot or online traffic, as most customers in this time period are actively shopping for the holidays.

19.3 Around the world

Small Business Saturday UK began in the UK in 2013 after the success of Small Business Saturday in America.*[8]

19.4 References

[1] ""Small Business Saturday" Campaign Boosts City Merchants". NY1 News. November 27, 2010.

[2] Mastrull, Diane (November 21, 2010). "In holiday shopping, Small Business Saturday is small business' rebuttal to Black Friday".

[3] Pena, Michel (November 27, 2010). " 'Small Business Saturday' ". StockBriefings.com.

[4] "North Carolina's small businesses noted as Gov. Perdue proclaims 'Small Business Saturday'". Associated Press. November 27, 2010.

[5] "Bloomberg promotes 'Small Business Saturday'". Associated Press. November 8, 2010.

[6] Dolak, Kevin (November 27, 2010). "Local Retailers Hope for Big Returns on Small Business Saturday". ABC News.

[7] "AmEx touts success of 'Small Business Saturday'". *U-T San Diego*. Retrieved 2 December 2014.

[8] "Small Business Saturday Hailed as Success. The Telegraph. 8 December 2013". *Telegraph.co.uk*. 8 December 2013. Retrieved 2 December 2014.

19.5 External links

- Facebook page
- US Small Business Administration

Chapter 20

Super Saturday

In the United Kingdom, "Super Saturday" refers to Day 8 of the 2012 Summer Olympics, when the U.K. recorded its most successful day at the Olympics in 104 years.

Super Saturday or **Panic Saturday** is the last Saturday before Christmas, a major day of revenue for American retailers, marking the end of the shopping season they and many customers believe begins on Black Friday. Super Saturday targets last-minute shoppers. Typically the day is ridden with one-day sales in an effort to accrue more revenue than any other day in the Christmas and holiday season.*[1]

20.1 Sales

Super Saturday typically nets approximately $15 billion in retail sales.*[2] To compete with each other, stores offer significant discounts and extend store hours in an attempt to attract customers and drive impulse buying.*[3]

Super Saturday accounts for a significant portion of the holiday sales for retail stores. In 2006, a study determined that sales between December 21 and 24 accounted for 13.6 percent of holiday sales.*[4] (In 2006, Super Saturday fell on December 23.) Some businesses do as much as 60 percent of their sales on this day.*[5]

In an effort to attract customers, stores often extend their hours during these crucial days of the retail season. Some stores go as far as to leave their stores open all day long until Christmas Eve in hopes that customers will take the extra time during off-peak hours to both review alternative options and to spread out workloads for cashiers.*[4] Because stores predict double or triple their typical customer turnout on Super Saturday, many increase their staffing during these critical days to be able to handle the demand.*[6]

20.2 Shoppers

The day typically nets a significant amount of revenue for retailers because of the demand by shoppers. 2009 reports indicated that by the middle of December, more than half of all shoppers in the United States still had more holiday shopping to do.*[7] Some experts predicted that approximately 40% of consumers hadn't started their holiday shopping by Super Saturday in 2009, with some customers citing full-time jobs as impeding their access to stores earlier in the year.*[6] Cathy Bergh from The Christmas House notes that the day is significant because it is "the last chance [for shoppers] to get out and do their shopping." *[1]

Some shoppers, however, intentionally wait for Super Saturday to finish their shopping due to the availability of discounts. Alternative reasons for waiting until the final Saturday to make holiday purchases include ensuring that purchases are within budget. Other customers choose to do their shopping early in an attempt to avoid the long lines and large crowds associated with the retail holiday.*[7]

Unlike Black Friday, online shopping does not typically infringe upon retail stores' access to customers. Due to Super Saturday's proximity to Christmas, shoppers are typically reluctant to venture online for deals, as purchases may not be able to arrive in time for the holiday.*[2] However, this is not always the case. If customers are unable to gain access to the stores, like what happened during the North American blizzard of 2009, customers who have little time left to buy their gifts may be forced online.*[8]

20.3 Other usages

Super Saturday can also be used for any Saturday where a large number of related events are held. In the context of the Eurovision Song Contest for example, the Saturday on which most broadcasters organize their national final is often declared as Super Saturday.*[9]

The final Saturday of the US Open in tennis is called "Super Saturday". If the tournament is running to schedule and has not been delayed by inclement weather or similar, both the men's semi-finals and the women's final are played on this day, with the men's semi-finals in the afternoon, then the women's final at night.

The phrase was also used (mainly by the British media) to refer to the middle Saturday of the 2012 Summer Olympics (4 August) where Team GB athletes Jessica Ennis, Mo Farah, Greg Rutherford, Danielle King, Laura Trott, Joanna Rowsell, Tom James, Pete Reed, Andrew Triggs-Hodge, Katherine Copeland and Sophie Hosking all won gold medals.

20.4 See also

- Cyber Monday

- Black Friday (shopping)

20.5 References

[1] Nick Natario. "Holiday Shoppers Pack Stores on Super Saturday". WETM TV. Retrieved 16 June 2010.

[2] Sy, Stephanie; Herman, Charles; Francescani, Chris. "Will Blizzard Blow Away Sales?". ABC News. Retrieved 20 December 2009.

[3] "Black Friday returns today for procrastinators". The Dallas Morning News. Retrieved 20 December 2009.

[4] Nicole Maestri (21 December 2007). "Stores desperately seeking shoppers on Super Saturday". Reuters. Retrieved 20 December 2009.

[5] John Carney. "Winter Storm Threatens to Bury "Super Saturday"". Business Insider. Retrieved 20 December 2009.

[6] Alcides Segui. "Super Saturday". Retrieved 16 June 2010.

[7] The KFBB News Team. "Super Saturday Shopping". KFBB News. Retrieved 20 December 2009.

[8] Dodes, Rachel; Zimmerman, Ann (20 December 2009). "Snowstorm Threatens 'Super Saturday' Sales". The Wall Street Journal. Retrieved 20 December 2009.

[9] "Mark it down: Super Saturday is this weekend".

Chapter 21

What Would Jesus Buy?

What Would Jesus Buy? is 2007 a documentary film produced by Morgan Spurlock and directed by Rob VanAlkemade. The title is a take-off on the phrase "What would Jesus do?" The film debuted on the festival circuit on March 11, 2007, at the South By Southwest (SXSW) conference in Austin, Texas. It went into general US release on November 16, 2007.*[1]

21.1 Plot

The film focuses on the issues of the commercialization of Christmas, materialism, the over-consumption in American culture, globalization, and the business practices of large corporations, as well as their economic and cultural effects on American society, as seen through the prism of activist/performance artist Bill Talen, who goes by the alias of "Reverend Billy", and his troupe of activists, whose street theater performances take the form of a church choir called "The Church of Stop Shopping," that sings anti-shopping and anti-corporate songs. The film follows Billy and his choir as they take a cross-country trip in the month prior to Christmas 2005, and spread their message against what they perceive as the evils of patronizing the retail outlets of several different large corporate chains.

21.2 Crew

The film was produced by Morgan Spurlock, with cinematography by Alan Deutsch, Daniel Marracino, Martin Palafox, Alex Stikich and Rob VanAlkemade. Jeremy Osbern was an additional cinematographer and Michael Moore, Dietmar Post, Jon Shenk, and Martin Taylor were camera operators. The film was edited by Gavin Coleman and Stela Georgieva.

21.3 Cast

- Adetola Abiade ... Alto

- Paul Allen ... Tenor

- Paul Norman Allen ... Paul

- Paul Norman Allen ... Tenor

- Shannon Baxter ... Soprano

- Rick Becker ... Trombone

- James Solomon Benn ... Choir Director / Choreographer

- Reverend Billy ... Reverend Billy

- Ben Cerf ... Bass

- Misun Choi ... Soprano

- Ben Dubin-Thaler ... Bass

- Savitri Durkee ... Church Director

- Leah Farrell ... Tenor

- Gina Figueroa ... Alto

- Mike Flthye ... Drums

21.4   See also

- Buy Nothing Christmas

- Buy Nothing Day

- Festivus

21.5   References

[1] Information on *What Would Jesus Buy?* at ioncinema.com

21.6   External links

- Official site

- *What Would Jesus Buy?* at the Internet Movie Database

- *What Would Jesus Buy?* at Rotten Tomatoes

- *What Would Jesus Buy?* at Metacritic

- *What Would Jesus Buy?* at AllMovie

- Church Of Stop Shopping

21.7 Text and image sources, contributors, and licenses

21.7.1 Text

- **Black Friday (shopping)** *Source:* https://en.wikipedia.org/wiki/Black_Friday_(shopping)?oldid=689381823 *Contributors:* Damian Yerrick, Bryan Derksen, Deb, Modemac, Edward, Kchishol1970, Greenman, Tregoweth, Sbuckley, Ahoerstemeier, Docu, Kingturtle, Julesd, Scott, Schneelocke, Ehn, Jengod, Timwi, Radiojon, Mattworld, JonathanDP81, Cvaneg, Dale Arnett, Justo, Friedo, Kizor, Rholton, Auric, LGagnon, Walloon, Xanzzibar, Mattflaschen, Dina, Radagast, Jwinters, Michael2, Giftlite, Smjg, Cattac, Tom harrison, Everyking, Iceberg3k, Bobblewik, Geni, Slowking Man, Antandrus, HorsePunchKid, Patrickjolliffe, Ary29, Qiq~enwiki, GreenReaper, D6, Jayjg, O'Dea, Aralvarez, Discospinster, Rich Farmbrough, Rhobite, Smyth, Tutwabee, Vitamin b, Bender235, Calamarain, Petersam, Evice, El C, Surachit, TheHungryTiger, Remember, Vipul, Jpgordon, Adambro, Bobo192, Stesmo, Hurricane111, Sortior, Viriditas, Jag123, I9Q79oL78KiL0QTFHgyc, JZH, Jhd, Alansohn, Gary, Ben James Ben, Mmmready, Great Scott, Shepd, Teucer, BRW, RJFJR, Geraldshields11, Mattbrundage, Loren, Markaci, Meadowbrook, Dennis Bratland, Tariqabjotu, Mahanga, Angr, Kelly Martin, Woohookitty, Nuggetboy, Uncle G, Lifung, Commander Keane, Kmg90, SCEhardt, Zzyzx11, Mandarax, Graham87, Spot Color Process, Rjwilmsi, Tim!, Nightscream, Koavf, Hairymon, FutureNJGov, Vegaswikian, Mecandes, The wub, Anskas, Gurch, Alphachimp, Nsteinberg, MrConstantin, Mercury McKinnon, YurikBot, Wavelength, RussBot, Manicsleeper, Rsrikanth05, Gustavb, NawlinWiki, Tvtonightokc, Kvn8907, JDoorjam, Retired username, Scottru, Dpparekh, Silverwind, PonyToast, Falcon9x5, Fun Guy Fungi, Caspian, Crumley, BazookaJoe, FF2010, Kawika, Icydesign, Arthur Rubin, Pb30, Livitup, Messy Thinking, MrBook, Back ache, Thespian, ManekiNeko, John Broughton, KKL, Tom Morris, SmackBot, Elonka, Va girl2468, MyrddinEmrys, CSMR, Moeron, J-beda, CRKingston, C.Fred, Davewild, Jstohler, Doc Strange, Exukvera, Brossow, HalfShadow, Mauls, Jmendez, Richmeister, Gilliam, DividedByNegativeZero, Hmains, Bradolson, Heckofit, Bluebot, GoldDragon, Caldorwards4, Too Human, Calliopejen~enwiki, MrNonchalant, Thumperward, SchfiftyThree, Hooriaj, Kostmo, Suicidalhamster, SolidVersed, Tartan, Rrburke, Rsm99833, Midnightcomm, Ortzinator, Cybercobra, Morr, Kevlar67, Derek R Bullamore, Dan Parnell, Ithizar, BigBadSanta, Ohconfucius, CIS, Weatherman1126, Delphii, ArglebargleIV, Rexhammock, General Ization, Timbudtwo, J 1982, Loodog, Gobonobo, IronGargoyle, Tiki God, Aerotive, Hvn0413, SQGibbon, Waggers, Citicat, Yoda4peace, Amitch, Vlad788, BranStark, Iridescent, TwistOfCain, Sebsmoot, Wake102, Bobamnertiopsis, Courcelles, Thomm1622, Gekaap, RattleandHum, BruceGrubb, Dycedarg, Linda robinett, Woudloper, Shyran, Toropop, John M Baker, Saffran, Cydebot, Karimarie, Dynamic1, Jdbsa05, Pdxuser, Shirulashem, DumbBOT, BhaiSaab, Frankcardoza, Tom Randolph, Epbr123, Dasani, Sarner, Keraunos, Sobreira, Marek69, TheTruthiness, Jbl1975, X96lee15, Silver Edge, AntiVandalBot, Seaphoto, Czj, Smartse, LibLord, JAnDbot, Canadiana, MER-C, Skomorokh, Kshuyler, Matthew Fennell, Fetchcomms, OLP1999, Dlwh, Wealjays, Y2kcrazyjoker4, AshwiniKalantri, Bencherlite, Magioladitis, Wikisofia, Johnelwaq, Bongwarrior, Timhood, JamesBWatson, Jay Gatsby, Sarahj2107, BobTheMad, Nyttend, Froid, Fleagle11, Beansy, Mjrmtg, Theroadislong, Jwikipro, Huseyx2, Quixotic Rick, JMyrleFuller, ArmadilloFromHell, JaGa, Cloudz679, Kirkjerk, Bertramanda, Lu33, Jidelawal, Lady Mondegreen, Cedian, Flowanda, Webinvestor, Gbcue, Wiki-mod~enwiki, Moggie2002, Cha5on, Arjun01, WotherspoonSmith, R'n'B, CommonsDelinker, 007kz, Bokbok, Timmmahhhh, HarZim, J.delanoy, Richiekim, SemDem, Jreferee, Katalaveno, McSly, Nemo bis, Little Professor, Victuallers, New Hampshirite, Sfphotocraft, Skier Dude, Keizers, Thug3, AntiSpamBot, GhostPirate, DeanHarding, Quantling, Inogenius, Student7, Juliancolton, Evb-wiki, Tiggerjay, Pbaez, Smeans2, Forhall, He Who Laughs Last~enwiki, Bonadea, Billyjobilly, Echosmoke, Deblock1376, Caspian blue, That-Vela-Fella, ABF, Jeff G., Butwhatdoiknow, Ryan032, Epson291, Philip Trueman, IRiteGood, TXiKiBoT, Kip the Dip, Atarisnerd, Njbob, Henryodell, Onore Baka Sama, Triesault, Enviroboy, Atlas1977, Vchimpanzee, Seresin, Neiltheslayer, Habbywall, Nagy, Kehrbykid, Logan, Legoktm, Pgerrity, Elisa Woods, SieBot, Coffee, 108Reliant, Dough4872, Laoris, Caltas, RJaguar3, Yintan, Theaveng, MaynardClark, Bsherr, Oxymoron83, Fimbriata, SilverbackNet, Elmyr, SimonTrew, Kav2001c, Jruderman, Kylehuegel, Spitfire19, DragonZero, EveryDayJoe45, Gdola, RegentsPark, SlackerMom, Martarius, Elassint, MaxForce, ClueBot, Mariordo, Hstevens86, Foxj, Theseven7, Arakunem, MyBigFatButt, Drmies, Yoshi Canopus, Robby.is.on, SuperHamster, CounterVandalismBot, Niceguyedc, Blanchardb, Dylan620, Myounesi, Trivialist, TimmmmCam, DragonBot, Marlow10, Excirial, Alexbot, Jusdafax, Coralmizu, Deathkenli, Gaff1229, Jls038, Dotforward, NuclearWarfare, Gemini 925, Narpole, Kaiba, Redthoreau, Curious Blue, Ark25, Fdg812000, Conmiro, Trulystand700, LightAnkh, XLinkBot, Let99, Duncan, Dthomsen8, Ost316, WikiRedactor, WikiHead, Doc9871, NellieBly, Swazland, Common Good, Kbdankbot, Addbot, Offenbach, Some jerk on the Internet, Fyrael, Coupcoup, Ronhjones, TutterMouse, Ironholds, CanadianLinuxUser, Fluffernutter, Blue Square Thing, Wikipedian314, Download, Proxima Centauri, Glane23, Jasper Deng, Tide rolls, Lightbot, Zorrobot, Arbitrarily0, MJEH, Luckas-bot, Yobot, Fraggle81, TaBOT-zerem, ScrewTheRules, Bigg3469, Dmarquard, AnomieBOT, RanEagle, Jim1138, JackieBot, Joeloop, AdjustShift, Ulric1313, Bluerasberry, Materialscientist, Aznboyarde, MrCodeDude, LilHelpa, Xqbot, Alexlange, Capricorn42, Khajidha, 4twenty42o, TechBot, Frscght, Gilo1969, Fancy steve, J4lambert, Anna Frodesiak, AuthorityTam, Abc kop l, SweynAsleiffson, NocturneNoir, Bliljerk101, OJSlaughter, Shirik, Jwojdylo, Uptodateinfo, Eugene-elgato, SD5, Dan6hell66, FrescoBot, MISTYFAN4EVER8887, Dogposter, HJ Mitchell, El Kael, CanadianNine, HamburgerRadio, GeneLesterisaMan, Pinethicket, Jonesey95, Spidey104, Calmer Waters, BigDwiki, Fat&Happy, Rotorcowboy, Meaghan, Leapday, DReifGalaxyM31, Xaethon, Designate, Tim1357, TobeBot, Lotje, Vrenator, Digitallib, Aoidh, Warrah, Agent-marge, Diannaa, ChronoKinetic, Zidanie5, Minimac, Pi zza314159, RjwilmsiBot, Ltt26, Bento00, Alph Bot, Joshritchie, Ripchip Bot, Tekgeek09, Sportstdh, Phlegat, Beyond My Ken, Dinidj, DannoNZ, Becritical, Billare, EmausBot, WikitanvirBot, Gfoley4, Tinss, Ebe123, S01310, RideReallyFlyball, JameyBM, TheSoundAndTheFury, Slightsmile, Mmeijeri, Wikipelli, K6ka, QueryOne, Trickytruck, MikeyMouse10, AvicBot, ZéroBot, Illegitimate Barrister, Truthsort, KuduIO, Lacon432, Hazard-SJ, SporkBot, Wayne Slam, L Kensington, Jorm (WMF), Donner60, Jackflash23, B Taylor-Blake, Tdowns14, ChuispastonBot, Iaagteacher, Manytexts, Pokbot, Davey2010, Gomacs, Howard035, PrivacyT, ClueBot NG, OmniRaden, Baron von Rassilon, Klicka8333, Ninedotnine, Gareth Griffith-Jones, Jack Greenmaven, Ahinks, Bped1985, Doug Grinbergs, Vacation9, Feedintm, ElvisFan1967, O.Koslowski, Widr, Antiqueight, Alacahanli, HMSSolent, Nongubpalm, Rockchalk717, Lowercase sigmabot, BG19bot, Z.graber, ElphiBot, MusikAnimal, Mark Arsten, Cschoolland, Fairlyoddparents1234, ThatEveningSun, C0mplex123, Caypartisbot, Rickyony, Wordx, BattyBot, Tutelary, Darylgolden, NWRGeek, ChrisGualtieri, GoShow, CrunchySkies, Br'er Rabbit, Mogism, Lugia2453, ProfessorTofty, Frosty, Rlehmann, BruceME, Constant pursuit, MattJasonBrown, Epicgenius, Daniel Sant'Anna Lisbôa, Merhaba1, Infinirex, Disk piss, Board nine, I am One of Many, Dairhead, Limefrost Spiral, Tentinator, Everymorning, EllenCT, Byung do jung, 00prometheus, Carl-northwood, Mariatim, Ginsuloft, KhushbooVira, Jackmcbarn, Askyourdoctor, Theking224, Mhohner, Arikk507, SimilarName, Ncchild, Yongsiriwat, Edwardnew, Dylan Jacob, Lmuston, Fortuna Imperatrix Mundi, Epic Failure, Holichick137, Deej4588, ModernSportsEra, Rev.DanielBeard, KingOfKoalas, Leegrc, Wattkins, Rehsjntdz, Andy012, GeoffreyT2000, Alxtye, Julunair, 33illuminati666, KH-1, Duncanr8, Journitecture, Dnivi3, Petrik121, Orduin, EnricoPallazzo1, Benjaminalvey, Martinireland23, Flying Squirrelzzz,

Wikikikikikikikikikikiikki, DariusDicks, Kookdcts, Mjk1234, Amorenor73, PeterDK, Thenapoleonchicken, Stevendw, Zouhourhalawi, Luuklp, Theoriginalhistorian, J.ahmad6, Timothy kwok share007, 3thmoon4, Andersonch10, TheABTHAN, Zoe1n only, Clazzhe, Iim batma, Lisa012, Retardundo and Anonymous: 961

- **Black Friday (South Park)** *Source:* https://en.wikipedia.org/wiki/Black_Friday_(South_Park)?oldid=685981056 *Contributors:* Nightscream, Koavf, McPhail, Hoof Hearted, Fractyl, Scorpion0422, DefLeppardVanHalen, DumbBOT, Froid, Edward321, Flyer22 Reborn, Correctonator, ImageRemovalBot, Martarius, Mezigue, Trivialist, Djole 555, Fortdj33, Cnwilliams, Grapesoda22, Canuckian89, Tbhotch, Mondotta, John of Reading, Charlesaaronthompson, Mikhail Ryazanov, ClueBot NG, (. j) a r g o n e l l e, Crazyboy279, Dewy60, Favre1fan93, Koopatrev, Matt723star, SNUGGUMS, Godwin1996, Mr.Gumby 531 and Anonymous: 8
- **Black Friday Sale** *Source:* https://en.wikipedia.org/wiki/Black_Friday_Sale?oldid=657966433 *Contributors:* Blightsoot, Derek R Bullamore, Dthomsen8, Blaylockjam10, Yobot, Cnwilliams, BattyBot, EnricoPallazzo1 and Anonymous: 1
- **Buy Nothing Christmas** *Source:* https://en.wikipedia.org/wiki/Buy_Nothing_Christmas?oldid=650980279 *Contributors:* SmackBot, Beetstra, Icedteapitcher, CalendarWatcher, Funandtrvl, Fences and windows, Jocamero, Randy Kryn, ClueBot, XLinkBot, AnomieBOT, FrescoBot, MattJasonBrown, There, I have an account and Anonymous: 13
- **Buy Nothing Day** *Source:* https://en.wikipedia.org/wiki/Buy_Nothing_Day?oldid=682192822 *Contributors:* LA2, SimonP, David spector, R Lowry, Mrwojo, Patrick, Kchishol1970, Liftarn, Minesweeper, Pcb21, Tregoweth, TheEternalVortex, Vzbs34, Emperorbma, Head, Denelson83, Altenmann, Romanm, Puckly, Meelar, Radagast, Peruvianllama, Wwoods, Darrien, Andycjp, Beland, Ary29, Esperant, Atlastawake, Rich Farmbrough, Szczym, Mwanner, Cretog8, Officiallyover, Zellin, Jumbuck, Inky, Dudenas, Jackliddle, Mattbrundage, Japanese Searobin, Zntrip, Angr, Woohookitty, Uncle G, Chochopk, Isnow, Zzyzx11, Graham87, Canderson7, Dubkiller, Misternuvistor, The wub, FlaBot, Freddydesouza, The Rambling Man, YurikBot, Wavelength, Rob T Firefly, SluggoOne, Lar, Hydrargyrum, Wiki alf, Nirvana2013, ONEder Boy, MaxVeers, Evrik, Zzuuzz, ChrisGriswold, SzymonSpengler~enwiki, JLaTondre, Lawyer2b, Jmchuff, SmackBot, Davepape, Eskimbot, Cacuija, Smeggysmeg, Bluebot, Iain.dalton, BabuBhatt, A. B., Mladifilozof, Can't sleep, clown will eat me, Krich, Ericbritton, Quatloo, Comrade Sephiroth, MusicMaker5376, John, Hannes Agnarsson Johnson, Ringmaster j, J 1982, Gobonobo, TheBenignBovine, Stearnsbrian, KokomoNYC, Esurnir, Bine maya, Danlev, Samuell, Wikipediarules2221, Doodleface, Mattisse, Davidmack, Dermo69, Aspensti, Daryl Thomas, Vulcanhacker, Waterthedog, Arsenikk, Skomorokh, Professor London, Some thing, Sarahj2107, Jim Douglas, Sangeet on Wikipedia, Cilstr, D.h, Icedteapitcher, Akbeancounter, Jmayoff, Huskier, White 720, Bonadea, Funandtrvl, Burlywood, VolkovBot, Cadby Waydell Bainbrydge, Fences and windows, Philip Trueman, Jacob Lundberg, Anna Lincoln, Munci, SieBot, MuzikJunky, Crackerjack, Yoda317, BotMultichill, CaelumArisen, Veggiedog, Denisarona, Randy Kryn, WikipedianMarlith, Faithlessthewonderboy, Sathiyamor, Spandrawn, Lucretius99, Niceguyedc, Rhododendrites, Let99, Kbdankbot, Addbot, Alternatevil, Glane23, AndersBot, Tide rolls, Cmano13, Kuzetsa, Luckasbot, Yobot, AnomieBOT, Lbercovitch, ChildofMidnight, Lightning Thundercat, Scandza, Skyerise, RedBot, Jbpayton, Clarkcj12, Diannaa, CatDevRandom, Guerillero, Freckletini, Lilyestelle, Gmichelle, Derrikaw, EmausBot, Wikiturrican, ZéroBot, Wayne Slam, Fturco, ClueBot NG, Raglankm, Phoenixred, Tilwednesday, Car Henkel, ISTB351, Wiki13, Cyj9176, C0mplex123, Jakobdegazio, Snowflake33, Oleg-ch, CrunchySkies, Impinball, TylerSymes, Jamez1502, Paradiise, Leegrc, Puppy9000, The Quixotic Potato and Anonymous: 189
- **Christmas club** *Source:* https://en.wikipedia.org/wiki/Christmas_club?oldid=628820463 *Contributors:* Jengod, Longhair, Woohookitty, Robert K S, Chochopk, Zzyzx11, Rjwilmsi, Ewlyahoocom, Airodyssey, SmackBot, Nbarth, Alaibot, Hillbillygirl, Mark Staffieri, Propaniac, Froid, Phoogenb, Mandsford, Sean.hoyland, Trivialist, Lightbot, Worm That Turned, FrescoBot, Full-date unlinking bot, GoingBatty, Captain Conundrum, MrLinkinPark333 and Anonymous: 6
- **Christmas creep** *Source:* https://en.wikipedia.org/wiki/Christmas_creep?oldid=688775472 *Contributors:* Kchishol1970, Zanimum, Julesd, Jengod, Grendelkhan, Bearcat, JackofOz, Pne, 159753, Andycjp, Xezbeth, Remember, Walter Görlitz, Zzyzx11, NeonMerlin, EamonnPKeane, Jimp, RussBot, Hydrargyrum, Tony1, Katana Geldar, Arthur Rubin, SmackBot, Hmains, Bluebot, J. Spencer, Rolypolyman, Vusys, Comrade Sephiroth, WayKurat, Redeagle688, Riffic, AlbertSM, Ibadibam, Otto4711, Serpent's Choice, OLP1999, Nyttend, JMyrleFuller, Dhaluza, Juliancolton, Abd4253, Enviroboy, Calliopejen1, Lightmouse, Artaxerxes, Some jerk on the Internet, AnomieBOT, Materialscientist, Cedricthecentaur, Full-date unlinking bot, Andymcgrath, Gardner356, GoingBatty, Thoroughgoodness, BG19bot, JohnChrysostom, MiffTheFox, BattyBot, ChrisGualtieri, Khazar2, MattJasonBrown, Amyp1023, IzzyMarlea and Anonymous: 34
- **Christmas Day (Trading) Act 2004** *Source:* https://en.wikipedia.org/wiki/Christmas_Day_(Trading)_Act_2004?oldid=544239661 *Contributors:* Edward, Gabbe, Jengod, Astrotrain, Mervyn, Andy, Bobblewik, Remember, Kurando, RussBot, Mais oui!, SmackBot, Bigbluefish, Slj, Neil Jones, Cydebot, Road Wizard, Bridgeplayer, Juliancolton, Warrior4321, Addbot, DisillusionedBitterAndKnackered, James500, Tom and sawyer lol, ZéroBot, Helpful Pixie Bot, MattJasonBrown and Anonymous: 4
- **Christmas Price Index** *Source:* https://en.wikipedia.org/wiki/Christmas_Price_Index?oldid=689126410 *Contributors:* Bewildebeast, Jengod, Gidonb, Peter Ellis, Andycjp, PFHLai, Clubjuggle, Rich Farmbrough, Dagonet, Nandhp, Walter Görlitz, H2g2bob, Rjwilmsi, Snek01, SmackBot, Quidam65, Jgera5, Noir~enwiki, Ser Amantio di Nicolao, JayHenry, Fvasconcellos, ShelfSkewed, Reywas92, Magioladitis, McDoobAU93, Juliancolton, Squids and Chips, PlaysInPeoria, Joseph A. Spadaro, JMOprof, Randy Kryn, RTaptap, SchreiberBike, Legobot, Myskills, Full-date unlinking bot, Trappist the monk, Jonkerz, RjwilmsiBot, K6ka, H3llBot, Helpful Pixie Bot, Luxure, Pipecork and Anonymous: 16
- **Cyber Black Friday** *Source:* https://en.wikipedia.org/wiki/Cyber_Black_Friday?oldid=669218766 *Contributors:* Bearcat, D6, Vegaswikian, SmackBot, C.Fred, Nbarth, Cydebot, Epbr123, DGG, Paulmcdonald, Quantling, Jayarathina, Tofutwitch11, Cyberstories, Frietjes, BG19bot, Gsanchez2011, Mgunn21 and Anonymous: 8
- **Cyber Monday** *Source:* https://en.wikipedia.org/wiki/Cyber_Monday?oldid=688752973 *Contributors:* The Anome, Waveguy, Greenman, Ahoerstemeier, Docu, Jengod, Yudel, Jerzy, Dale Arnett, Patcat88, Enochlau, Bobblewik, R. fiend, Mzajac, OwenBlacker, EricKerby, Jareha, Paulmorriss, D6, AAAAA, Discospinster, Narsil, Alansohn, ReyBrujo, Versageek, Richard Arthur Norton (1958-), ^demon, Smmurphy, Tejastheory, Zzyzx11, Stefanomione, BD2412, Spot Color Process, Rjwilmsi, Tim!, Hairymon, Agiorgio, Vegaswikian, DVdm, Bgwhite, Jimp, Rsrikanth05, Bovineone, Anomalocaris, Daikiki, Currybet, ChrisGriswold, John Broughton, SmackBot, Chodges, KnowledgeOfSelf, Shoy, C.Fred, Lakeyboy, Cattus, Jprg1966, Giorces, Frankencow, Cattrain, Quokkapox, IronCityPerson, IronCityBeer, EmpyreanDraco, Drunken Pirate, CIS, John, Gobonobo, Robofish, JHunterJ, Dlandre, Andreworkney, Marsnoir, HelloAnnyong, Toropop, Mt1955, Cydebot, Torc2, DumbBOT, Chrislk02, Sparklenight, JAF1970, Epbr123, James086, Oreo Priest, Czj, Smartse, Nipisiquit, Skomorokh, Y2kcrazyjoker4,

GrimbleGrumble, Scanlan, Telanis, Antientropic, Froid, Bostoner, Mjrmtg, Gbcue, Ryper, Sawblade5, JammingEcono, Tgeairn, Skier Dude, Sbrobin, Yanks-rule, Quantling, Bonadea, Enivid, VolkovBot, Epson291, Rich Janis, Falcon8765, Vchimpanzee, StAnselm, Demantos, Meeinter, EveryDayJoe45, Denisarona, Jonm839, Martarius, ClueBot, Barbabob~enwiki, Rodhullandemu, Vivio Testarossa, Jaericho, Bankerva, Horselover Frost, Let99, MystBot, Wyatt915, Addbot, Teafragger, Kelly, Offenbach, Some jerk on the Internet, 2ndAmendment, SpBot, Tide rolls, Gwf28, Yobot, Worm That Turned, MrBlueSky, Tflash2612, AnomieBOT, Calcobrena, ARDink, Citation bot, Mononomic, Gilo1969, Guruzazu, Shirik, Jwojdylo, Locobot, FrescoBot, Hexafluoride, Mimzy1990, Spidey104, Skyerise, Meaghan, Pristino, GGBiscuit, Danifronter, Trappist the monk, Lotje, Tofutwitch11, Vrenator, Staffordj14, Logical Fuzz, Mean as custard, RjwilmsiBot, Love149, Nougat77, El43453, J36miles, EmausBot, LeoLavish, Dewritech, Wikipelli, Trickytruck, MattCuts, John Cline, Fæ, SporkBot, Sky380, NYMets2000, L Kensington, Carmichael, MurphEngineer, Rocketrod1960, ClueBot NG, Jack Greenmaven, Ikellenberger, Scrap213, Frietjes, Dreth, AgniKalpa, Widr, BG19bot, Davidhaymond, MusikAnimal, Mark Arsten, Loulounz, Nosson317, Gsanchez2011, Klilidiplomus, BattyBot, Norrobbins, Chris-Gualtieri, Mediran, SoledadKabocha, Webclient101, Little green rosetta, Razibot, Titanic2534, Tomlongshlong696969420, Pru26e, Tentinator, Mariatim, Mgunn21, Berri-UQAM, Richardbristol7, Cybermondaydeals, Leegrc, Maddie1996z, TerryAlex, GeoffreyT2000, KH-1, BobbyThomas43, Militto2015, Dellivehonor, Princessdedios, Carlrachman, Cocslat69, StealthyJoker85, AirPaki, Eric18880, Jaimkabra and Anonymous: 282

- **Economics of Christmas** *Source:* https://en.wikipedia.org/wiki/Economics_of_Christmas?oldid=667979720 *Contributors:* Walter Görlitz, Neelix, Dentren, JMyrleFuller, AnomieBOT, KH-1 and Anonymous: 4

- **El Buen Fin** *Source:* https://en.wikipedia.org/wiki/El_Buen_Fin?oldid=683229758 *Contributors:* Docu, D6, BD2412, Keizers, Addbot, AnomieBOT, EmausBot, MrNiceGuy1113, Hmainsbot1, Lizreyesk, MattJasonBrown, Aedicul and Anonymous: 11

- **Festivus** *Source:* https://en.wikipedia.org/wiki/Festivus?oldid=678230585 *Contributors:* The Cunctator, Bryan Derksen, Shsilver, SimonP, Zoe, Chuq, Frecklefoot, Infrogmation, Michael Hardy, Cprompt, Tregoweth, KAMiKAZOW, Ronz, Angela, Emperor, Julesd, Jeandré du Toit, Rawr, Jouster, John K, Jengod, Saint-Paddy, Dcoetzee, JonMoore, Stone, Tpbradbury, Ark30inf, Raul654, AnonMoos, Branddobbe, Dale Arnett, Kizor, Ektar, Justanyone, Idiotfromia, Auric, Catbar, JamesMLane, Sstair, Everyking, Jonabbey, Curps, SWAdair, Gyrofrog, Gadfium, Alexf, Telso, CryptoDerk, MarkSweep, Doops, Rdsmith4, Eranb, Grossdomestic, Goobergunch, Ukexpat, Lacrimosus, Rcv, MToolen, D6, Rich Farmbrough, Vsmith, Timsabin, Amoore, Bishonen, Aris Katsaris, Nard the Bard, MattTM, JoeSmack, Brian0918, Kaszeta, Livajo, Shmuel, Bdoserror, Lambertman, Clawson, Jmah, Spug, Raemie, Vanished user azby388723i8jfjh32, Googuse, Edheil, Alansohn, Gary, Andrewpmk, Jnothman, Eisensean, Cadre, Samaritan, Hu, Tancred, Dhartung, SidP, TaintedMustard, Omphaloscope, Harej, Henry W. Schmitt, Computerjoe, Walshga, Dismas, Muhgcee, Preost, Zntrip, HLacheen, Soultaco, Joelpt, Mel Etitis, OwenX, IRbaboon, GVOLTT, Peng~enwiki, Can'tStandYa, Skyraider, MrWhipple, Tomlillis, Wikiklrsc, Damicatz, Bluemoose, Toussaint, Liface, Shanedidona, Inic, Ashmoo, Graham87, Deltabeignet, Elliotharmon, Kalmia, Tovias, FantumGrey, Don Braffitt, BD2412, Bardnet, Levelistchampion, Schmendrick, Kane5187, Rjwilmsi, Makaristos, Netan'el, Bubba73, MarnetteD, MLRoach, Yamamoto Ichiro, CDThieme, Naraht, Alhutch, Patken4, Steveo2, Jdurbach, Ahunt, Deklund, Eraserhead1, Stan2525, Wikky Horse, Akamad, Grubber, Gaius Cornelius, Kyorosuke, Bovineone, Daniel Pritchard, Foxmulder, Howcheng, Nick, Dahveed323, EEMIV, Lucasreddinger, Cardsplayer4life, DRosenbach, Evrik, Lumaga, Casey Madeline, Shwirtz, Alarob, Whytee, Tokai, Thnidu, Nikkimaria, Arthur Rubin, Fang Aili, Careax, Ehlkej, Colmbuckley, GraemeL, Fram, Marco Passarani, Warreed, Darren Lee, Jeff Silvers, Finell, Wikichutney, True Pagan Warrior, SmackBot, FunnyYetTasty, Hkhenson, TracerBulIet, McGeddon, CantStandYa, Pgk, C.Fred, Brick Thrower, Frymaster, Brossow, Kintetsubuffalo, Inonit, Cheese3037, Nscheffey, Kuzmatt9, Hvn73, StarKruzr, Jporcaro, Ohnoitsjamie, Chris the speller, Jprg1966, Tree Biting Conspiracy, Sixhoursago, Polkapunk, No-Bullet, Aaron Solomon Adelman, Emurphy42, Iregretthisname, Tonyleto, Dethme0w, Ioscius, Zone46, MinuteHand, OrphanBot, Akrubin, Mmmmaaaacccckkkk, Ortzinator, Pastorwayne, Radagast83, BigBurkey, AndroidCat, RolandR, Vanished user iohfihw3i8i3hijkse, Tomtom9041, St4nst4n, TheST, Chopin Fanatic, Kendrick7, Magicballs69, Tricadex, J.smith, Wikipedical, Ace ETP, CIS, Skiasaurus, Esrever, Nishkid64, Stewie814, Sophia, Irstenstein, Filthish, Gobonobo, Mpanetta, KennyMan666, Morshem, Hulmem, Paradoxsociety, BillFlis, Special-T, TheHYPO, N1ghtstr1k3, Jamie King, SandyGeorgia, Ryanjunk, TJ Spyke, Norm mit, ChetTheGray, Pipedreambomb, Roadhockey, JoeBot, Shoeofdeath, Darth Borehd, Twas Now, Izaakb, Nortelrye, Namiba, Nastunya, EightyOne, Bubbha, Andreasjb, Ratman9999, HDCase, Betaeleven, Wordupvb08, CmdrObot, Endeavor51, Cmieuli, QuinnJL, Apterygial, Hypercritic, Ntsimp, CohibaX, Slp1, Phil in the 818, Mike Bags, Dreadpiratetif, Flowerpotman, Pascal.Tesson, Thaddius, DumbBOT, Jbrickell, MisterActually, Richhoncho, UV, InkQuill, JamesAM, Thijs!bot, Tthaas, Bbemis~enwiki, CheesemonkeyFrenchperson, Kathovo, Gopman1, Pmrobert49, Second Quantization, LateToTheGame, Rhrad, AgentPeppermint, Natalie Erin, KrakatoaKatie, AntiVandalBot, Dbrodbeck, MelonSmasher, Malcolm, *Mystic*, Darrenhusted, DOSGuy, NapoliRoma, Skomorokh, Seanbow, Vandymorgan, Dcooper, Tomorrow Never Knows, Some thing, RainbowCrane, VoABot II, AuburnPilot, Telanis, Jay Gatsby, Singularity, Jim Douglas, Allensalkin, Isaiahcambron, Animum, Maxpappagiorgio, C.Logan, KenThomas, Mac addict, Qohen, Whedonette, BMRR, Kiore, DesignOne, Uriel8, AlphaEta, StormXor, Khurg100, UBeR, TV Tony, MatthewKosmoski, SemDem, PRB216, Cocoaguy, Jerry, Thaurisil, AmericanPie07, Captain Infinity, McSly, Naniwako, Clurd1, Ben1283, Rev. John, ULC, Flatterworld, Jgroub, Duffelmeier, Remember the dot, King Toadsworth, Feats-O-Strength, Psdubow, Smoothrat, Esjayel, Will Yums, Deblock1376, X!, Malik Shabazz, Ancient ancestor, Patski762, Dcr248, TallNapoleon, Mhoneycutt11, Butwhatdoiknow, Snapshott22, Martinmott, Zhou yi777, Philip Trueman, Martinevans123, EricSerge, Xenophrenic, Epaphroditus Ph. M.~enwiki, Malinaccier, Jsgoodrich, Chaospaladin, Emigdioofmiami, Rjb12, Wiikipedian, Gekritzl, Joseph A. Spadaro, Softlavender, Rypcord, John Stattic, Chunk Champion, Iciac, This, that and the other, Crash Underride, Flyer22 Reborn, Joevibe, Rcnvr, Frank Anchor, LeoStarDragon1, MarkinBoston, Dabomb87, Dionysius525, Randy Kryn, Tomdobb, Invertzoo, Baseballfan789, Beeblebrox, ClueBot, Snigbrook, Mattgirling, Jeff Smoker, Bicycle legs, Piriczki, Boing! said Zebedee, Mezigue, Trivialist, Zoeydahling, Burt64nyg, DecaturHeel, Mr.Atoz, Music2611, MatttK, Clayt85, 842U, Danielokeefe, Porkman Pork, Project FMF, Mattp5127, Its UNBELIEVABLE, Versus22, Quicktrade, Thewiseeye3400, Jlomcc, Rudy2828, XLinkBot, Bradv, Dthomsen8, Alexius08, Valerie2776, Thebestofall007, Wyatt915, RKill, Addbot, MartinezMD, Reedmalloy, Proxima Centauri, Paravail, JoboG, Peridon, Dayewalker, Luckas Blade, Weaseloid, RichardBond, Mr.Vanker, Aric.bickel, Legobot, Luckas-bot, Yobot, Jason Recliner, Esq., AnomieBOT, DemocraticLuntz, Wrongfilter, Gavin Coles, Jim1138, Kennedy4200, Flamingeagle435, Citation bot, Eleventh Guard, LilHelpa, PoweredByLolcats, Aquila89, Nasnema, ChildofMidnight, Inferno, Lord of Penguins, Anonymous from the 21st century, Srobiche, Sittingonthefence, Geralddarden, Dimeesq, Pwitter, FrescoBot, Anna Roy, LucienBOT, Mcndogg, ZombieTed, Intelligentsium, Gfcvoice, Blargh29, Jonesey95, A8UDI, Tylerelliott, Jandalhandler, Full-date unlinking bot, Train2104, Fama Clamosa, Vrenator, Paulg 127, Ggnvol, Gardrek, Tbhotch, Minimac, RjwilmsiBot, Luhshawnda, Beyond My Ken, Bessdag, Cortina2, Koppapa, Charlesaaronthompson, RA0808, Trickytruck, Jc3h5s, Phancy, Gthya, H3llBot, 12b3, Wingman4l7, Erianna, Birthdayresearcher813, Δ, Ihardlythinkso, Mcc1789, Rsws, Will Beback Auto, ClueBot NG, BarrelProof, ESYoung, Darkthysal, Davypavy, Adam.a.segal, Helpful Pixie Bot, Calidum, Candleabracadabra, Emayv, Marcocapelle, Allecher,

Compfreak7, Johnny Squeaky, RadioEverleigh, MikeJ371, Sw2659001, Darkthistle, Pieceofmeat, EdenCole, Liam987, BigJolly9, Hmainsbot1, Wenjanglau, Mogism, Theoa, Wywin, Epicgenius, BKlaw2616, TheycallmetheDoctor, Warped War, Kramer is my Hero, Tondaror27, Flyingcat123, WikiDanoSD, Monkbot, Chrisswiggum, Cainka, Bagojunk, 4marknelson, Randall44 and Anonymous: 885

- **Giving Tuesday** *Source:* https://en.wikipedia.org/wiki/Giving_Tuesday?oldid=688801053 *Contributors:* Beland, Vipul, Josh3580, Jcarroll, Ser Amantio di Nicolao, Ceferlyj, Drmies, AnomieBOT, FrescoBot, Mean as custard, GoingBatty, CTF83! Alt, Dexbot, Leegrc, GivingTuesday, Caf research, Squaresandstuff, Giving Tuesday España and Anonymous: 6

- **Green Monday** *Source:* https://en.wikipedia.org/wiki/Green_Monday?oldid=675383369 *Contributors:* Andrewman327, Sysin, SidP, BDD, Gene Nygaard, Tim!, XP1, Asarelah, Nikkimaria, Sobreira, T L Miles, Fabrictramp, Huggi, Addbot, Skywalker122, Kwacka, AnomieBOT, RadioBroadcast, BlackKarasu, Alvb, Envirogeek, SporkBot, BG19bot, Mattdolge, Leegrc, KH-1, StealthyJoker85 and Anonymous: 9

- **Sears Wish Book** *Source:* https://en.wikipedia.org/wiki/Sears_Wish_Book?oldid=672580710 *Contributors:* Mustang dvs, SmackBot, Davewild, Thumperward, MarshBot, SkagitRiverQueen, PeterGriffin1940, Grundle2600, Trivialist, Lightbot, AnomieBOT, Tbhotch, Feedintm, Snotbot, Hmainsbot1, MattJasonBrown, ArmbrustBot, Riddleh and Anonymous: 11

- **Singles Day** *Source:* https://en.wikipedia.org/wiki/Singles_Day?oldid=655888656 *Contributors:* Chuunen Baka, Mushroom, Ukexpat, D6, Caesar, Bobo192, Harro5, Benlisquare, Bgwhite, RussBot, SmackBot, Cattus, Tim Ross, General Ization, Simonalexander2005, Cydebot, Nthep, Mkdw, CommonsDelinker, ASDFGH, Billydeeuk, Baosheng, ImageRemovalBot, Sfan00 IMG, ClueBot, Liuzhou, Alexbot, Hozo, XLinkBot, Addbot, Download, Luckas-bot, Yobot, Fraggle81, Ipatrol, CompliantDrone, Howchou, Skyerise, Kellyheuer07, Gelisam, John of Reading, Helpsome, ClueBot NG, Talentfish, Bucsong, Gao le, Northamerica1000, NNU-11-22100511, NNU-01-Zhu Xiaoxiao, Mingqiang Gu, Papoore, Shwangtianyuan, Jcrjcr, PhoenixDai, Febetsh23, Frosty, Liz Hongs, VeryCrocker, Blwikis, Chrionexfleckeri1350, Samwangwang, Bierebaron, Scottube, Nysrtup and Anonymous: 35

- **Small Business Saturday** *Source:* https://en.wikipedia.org/wiki/Small_Business_Saturday?oldid=689203914 *Contributors:* Bearcat, Dale Arnett, D6, Rich Farmbrough, Koavf, Mahalie, Jared Preston, Wavelength, Whoisjohngalt, Gaius Cornelius, Malcolma, Ser Amantio di Nicolao, Gobonobo, Dstruct2k, Quantling, KylieTastic, Wikidemon, Njbob, Trivialist, XLinkBot, Let99, AnomieBOT, Shadowjams, FrescoBot, Cinda Baxter, SporkBot, Matthewhantz, Surfguy1994, Leegrc, Cmsmallbiz and Anonymous: 17

- **Super Saturday** *Source:* https://en.wikipedia.org/wiki/Super_Saturday?oldid=667472784 *Contributors:* Docu, Jengod, Dale Arnett, YUL89YYZ, Madkayaker, Thumbling, CIS, DVD Smith, Aspirex, NativeForeigner, Woodshed, Jbitkill, Jimthing, Bradley0110, Addbot, Arbitrarily0, Yobot, LovesMacs, Jayarathina, Shirik, MISTYFAN4EVER8887, Tinton5, Abc518, Digitallib, RjwilmsiBot, ZéroBot, ByrdMan13, Manytexts, MasterMind5991, Khazar2, Mogism, Mrsybc and Anonymous: 9

- **What Would Jesus Buy?** *Source:* https://en.wikipedia.org/wiki/What_Would_Jesus_Buy%3F?oldid=666443507 *Contributors:* Alan Liefting, Andycjp, AliveFreeHappy, Xezbeth, Hagerman, Nightscream, Nickv111, Cardsplayer4life, JQF, Garion96, SmackBot, Forteller~enwiki, Rst20xx, Atropos, Ser Amantio di Nicolao, Grandpafootsoldier, Cydebot, Ajelectrowhiz, After Midnight, Khigh, Pixelface, ResurgamII, Mtjaws, MastCell, Rettetast, Aqwis, Shawn in Montreal, Mike V, Syndetic, Brooklyn m, Polbot, Thirteen squared, Randy Kryn, ClueBot, Leif.baradoy, Jarble, Full-date unlinking bot, Jonkerz, Eekerz, Terraflorin, Hmainsbot1 and Anonymous: 23

21.7.2 Images

- **File:Ambox_globe_content.svg** *Source:* https://upload.wikimedia.org/wikipedia/commons/b/bd/Ambox_globe_content.svg *License:* Public domain *Contributors:* Own work, using File:Information icon3.svg and File:Earth clip art.svg *Original artist:* penubag

- **File:Ambox_important.svg** *Source:* https://upload.wikimedia.org/wikipedia/commons/b/b4/Ambox_important.svg *License:* Public domain *Contributors:* Own work, based off of Image:Ambox scales.svg *Original artist:* Dsmurat (talk · contribs)

- **File:Calendar_icon.svg** *Source:* https://upload.wikimedia.org/wikipedia/commons/d/dd/Calendar_icon.svg *License:* CC-BY-SA-3.0 *Contributors:* Transferred from en.wikipedia; transferred to Commons by User:Lvova using CommonsHelper. *Original artist:* Original uploader was Vystrix Nexoth at en.wikipedia

- **File:ChristmasMarketJena.jpg** *Source:* https://upload.wikimedia.org/wikipedia/commons/4/45/ChristmasMarketJena.jpg *License:* CC BY-SA 2.0 *Contributors:* http://www.flickr.com/photos/rene-germany/2126809489/?addedcomment=1#comment72157611118374576 *Original artist:* ReneS at flickr

- **File:Christmas_Price_Index_(1984-2009).svg** *Source:* https://upload.wikimedia.org/wikipedia/commons/5/55/Christmas_Price_Index_%281984-2009%29.svg *License:* Public domain *Contributors:* Own work *Original artist:* Nandhp

- **File:Commons-logo.svg** *Source:* https://upload.wikimedia.org/wikipedia/en/4/4a/Commons-logo.svg *License:* ? *Contributors:* ? *Original artist:* ?

- **File:DCUSA.Gallery11.BB&BBlackFriday.Wikipedia.jpg** *Source:* https://upload.wikimedia.org/wikipedia/commons/7/7d/DCUSA.Gallery11.BB%26BBlackFriday.Wikipedia.jpg *License:* Public domain *Contributors:* Own work (Original text: *I (Gridprop (talk)) created this work entirely by myself.*) *Original artist:* Gridprop at English Wikipedia

- **File:Edit-clear.svg** *Source:* https://upload.wikimedia.org/wikipedia/en/f/f2/Edit-clear.svg *License:* Public domain *Contributors:* The *Tango! Desktop Project.* *Original artist:*
  The people from the Tango! project. And according to the meta-data in the file, specifically: "Andreas Nilsson, and Jakub Steiner (although minimally)."

- **File:Festivus_Meatloaf_on_a_bed_of_lettuce.JPG** *Source:* https://upload.wikimedia.org/wikipedia/commons/8/86/Festivus_Meatloaf_on_a_bed_of_lettuce.JPG *License:* CC BY-SA 4.0 *Contributors:* Own work *Original artist:* 4marknelson

- **File:Festivus_Pole.jpg** *Source:* https://upload.wikimedia.org/wikipedia/commons/7/79/Festivus_Pole.jpg *License:* CC BY 2.0 *Contributors:* Flickr: Celebrating Festivus 2 *Original artist:* Matthew Keefe

21.7.3   Content license

www.ingramcontent.com/pod-product-compliance
Lightning Source LLC
Chambersburg PA
CBHW082014290526
45787CB00016B/2694